UAE AND THE GULF

Architecture and Urbanism Now

ARCHITECTURAL DESIGN
January/February 2015
Profile No 233

Guest-Edited by
GEORGE KATODRYTIS
AND KEVIN MITCHELL

OMA, Qatar National Library, Education City, Doha, Qatar, 2014

RMJM Architects, Capital Gate, Abu Dhabi, UAE, 2011

ISSN 0003-8504
ISBN 978-1118-759066

Guest-edited by **George Katodrytis and Kevin Mitchell**

*'The expansion of cities
like Dubai and Doha
results in global media
attention that focuses
on the scale and speed
of growth; however,
characterisations are often
reduced to caricature,
which prohibits a more
nuanced understanding
of the forces that shape
architecture and
urbanism in the region.'
– George Katodrytis
and Kevin Mitchell*

Oil Tanks,
Dubai, UAE,
1969

Mangera Yvars
Architects (MYAA),
Qatar Faculty of
Islamic Studies
(QFIS) and Education
City Mosque,
Education City,
Doha, Qatar
2014

Editorial Offices
John Wiley & Sons
25 John Street
London WC1N 2BS
UK

T +44 (0)20 8326 3800

Editor
Helen Castle

Managing Editor (Freelance)
Caroline Ellerby

Production Editor
Elizabeth Gongde

Prepress
Artmedia, London

Art Direction + Design
CHK Design:
Christian Küsters
Sophie Troppmair

Printed in Italy by Printer
Trento Srl

Front cover: X-Architects
with BuroHappold, Darb
Al Mashaer Masterplan,
Makkah, Saudi Arabia,
2013. Image ©X-Architects.
Graphics by CHK Design

Inside front cover: Inside
front cover and page 1:
Manar Kamal,
[de]construction, collages
from Dubai, September
2013. © Manar Kamal

01 / 2015

MIX
Paper from
responsible sources
FSC® C015829

ARCHITECTURAL DESIGN

January/February
2015

Profile No.
233

Subscription Offices UK
John Wiley & Sons Ltd
Journals Administration Department
1 Oldlands Way, Bognor Regis
West Sussex, PO22 9SA, UK
T: +44 (0)1243 843 272
F: +44 (0)1243 843 232
E: cs-journals@wiley.com

Print ISSN: 0003-8504
Online ISSN: 1554-2769

Prices are for six issues and include postage and
handling charges. Individual-rate subscriptions must
be paid by personal cheque or credit card. Individual-
rate subscriptions may not be resold or used as
library copies.

All prices are subject to change without notice.

Identification Statement
Periodicals Postage paid at Rahway, NJ 07065.
Air freight and mailing in the USA by
Mercury Media Processing, 1850 Elizabeth Avenue,
Suite C, Rahway, NJ 07065, USA.

USA POSTMASTER: please send address changes to
Architectural Design, c/o Mercury Media Processing,
1634 E. Elizabeth Avenue, Linden, NJ 07036, USA.

Rights and Permissions
Requests to the Publisher should be addressed to:
Permissions Department
John Wiley & Sons Ltd
The Atrium
Southern Gate
Chichester
West Sussex PO19 8SQ
UK

F: +44 (0)1243 770 620
E: permreq@wiley.com

Subscribe to Ɑ
Ɑ is published bimonthly and is available to
purchase on both a subscription basis and as
individual volumes at the following prices.

Prices
Individual copies: £24.99 / US$45
Individual issues on Ɑ App
for iPad: £9.99 / US$13.99
Mailing fees for print may apply

Annual Subscription Rates
Student: £75 / US$117 print only
Personal: £120 / US$189 print and iPad access
Institutional: £212 / US$398 print or online
Institutional: £244 / US$457 combined
print and online
6-issue subscription on Ɑ App
for iPad: £44.99 / US$64.99

In the 2000s, the architecture of the UAE and the Gulf attracted international attention and widespread awe. This was epitomised by the audacity and the conspicuous opulence of luxury developments in Dubai such as the Palm Islands, artificial islands reclaimed from the ocean shaped in the form of palm trees; the 7-star sail-shaped Burj Al Arab Hotel (1999) designed by Tom Wright of Atkins, the highest hotel in the world; and SOM's Burj Khalifa (2010) in downtown Dubai, the tallest tower in the world. In the academic architecture community, the attention-grabbing impudence of these excesses was compounded by Dubai's upstart status as a new city that had risen out of the desert within decades – it was widely referred to as 'a phenomenon'. It became the popular focus of urban studies and student research trips. When I made a short visit to the UAE in the autumn of 2012, three years after Dubai experienced its financial crisis in 2009, it was apparent that the situation in the individual emirates and the Gulf was both more diverse and more complex than the stereotypical view that is commonly communicated. At the American University of Sharjah (AUS), the premier architecture school in the region, I was lucky enough to be introduced by the former Dean of the College of Architecture, Art and Design, Peter di Sabatino, to Professors George Katodrytis and Kevin Mitchell. A conversation was initiated with George and Kevin about how they might reframe the architectural and urban situation in the UAE for an issue of △ that would lead to the more 'nuanced' view outlined in their introduction that 'favours critique over caricature' (see pp 8–19).

EDITORIAL

HELEN CASTLE

The picture that George and Kevin and their contributors provide is a far cry from the bling of me-me Dubai architecture of the 2000s. Highlighting key issues such as the various manifestations of rapid urbanisation, the cultural identity of heritage and education buildings and sustainability, they bring the recent history and immediate future of the region under close scrutiny. By inviting Noura Al Sayeh, the Head of Architectural Affairs at the Ministry of Culture of the Kingdom of Bahrain, to write the Counterpoint for the issue, △ has looked even further into the crystal ball by daring to ask: What might happen when the oil runs out – oil having resourced most urban development across the region since the 1970s? Bahrain, unlike its neighbours, is already facing the depletion of oil resources, with the lowest reserves of all Gulf Cooperation Council (GCC) countries. What might be the drivers in a country like Bahrain for a new architecture that is primarily driven by concerns for economical and environmental sustainability? △

George Katodrytis
_____

Virus House
_____

Cyprus
_____

2001

Award-winning detached house
generated through a series of folds and
shifts exploring the plastic characteristics
of in-situ concrete. Surfaces and structure
are developed into a single geometric and
hybrid system.

George Katodrytis and
Sharmeen Syed
_____

Roaming Trans_cities and
Airborne Fiction
_____

Dubai, UAE
_____

2011

Proposal for an abandoned megaproject
landscape in the UAE. Reconnaissance
technologies in the Gulf turn into
spectacle and 'telegenic' fantasies.
Simulated panoramas and imagery
of unfinished projects give rise to an
exciting promise shaping the future of
cities.

Kevin Mitchell
_____

Courtyard Housing
_____

American University of
Sharjah campus
_____

Sharjah, UAE
_____

2003

Floor plan and exterior view of
courtyard housing designed for the
American University of Sharjah campus.
Incorporating principles found in regional
precedents, the project demonstrates
how courtyard models from the past can
be adapted to provide a contemporary
response to climate and context.

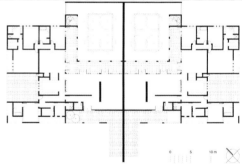

Kevin Mitchell
_____

Emirates Photography
Competition Exhibition
_____

Manarat Al Saadiyat
_____

Abu Dhabi, UAE
_____

2014

Conceived as a spatial landscape derived
from a reinterpretation of the structure
of formal gardens in the Islamic world,
the design for the Emirates Photography
Competition incorporated premiated
photographs from across the world and a
parallel exhibition showcasing work from
well-known photographers from the UAE,
Egypt and Bangladesh.

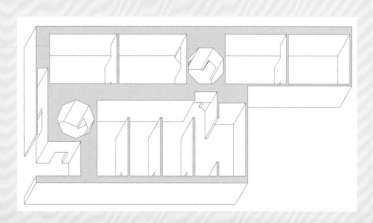

ABOUT THE
GUEST EDITORS

GEORGE KATODRYTIS AND
KEVIN MITCHELL

George Katodrytis and Kevin Mitchell teach at the American University of Sharjah (AUS) in the United Arab Emirates and they have been involved in joint projects for over 10 years. In addition to collaborating on research on the architecture and urbanism of the Gulf region, they have worked together on workshops and design studios in Jordan and Italy. They co-developed and co-teach a course entitled 'Shelter and Settlement in Post-Conflict Societies', and continue to collaborate on projects that address refugee-related issues.

George Katodrytis is an architect involved in practice, teaching and research. He is currently Associate Professor of Architecture at AUS. He studied and taught at the Architectural Association (AA) in London and has been a visiting professor at various schools around the world. He has worked in Paris, London, Nicosia and Dubai. He has built a number of projects in Europe and the Middle East, and published widely on contemporary architecture, urbanism, cultural theory and digital media. His work addresses the Gulf 'city', especially as it is evolving in the 21st century. He employs digital technology and scripting as tools for establishing new formal and performative language and fabrication in architecture. He is also involved in a series of design projects in territories of limited resources that include children's homes, schools and refugee camps in the Middle East and Africa.

Kevin Mitchell has taught at AUS since 1999 and currently serves as Interim Provost. Areas of research and writing include design pedagogy and contemporary architecture and urbanism in the Middle East. His recent work has appeared in *The Superlative City: Dubai and the Urban Condition in the Early Twenty-First Century* (Harvard University Press, 2013), *Architecture and Globalisation in the Persian Gulf Region* (Ashgate, 2013), *Transfigurations: Photographs of Tarek Al Ghoussein* (Black Dog Publishing, in press) and *The Courtyard House: Between Cultural Expression and Universal Application* (Ashgate, 2010). He is a founding Editorial Board member for the *International Journal of Islamic Architecture*. Ɒ

INTRODUCTION

GEORGE KATODRYTIS AND
KEVIN MITCHELL

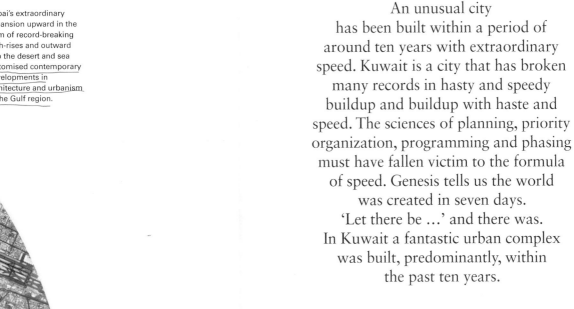

An unusual city
has been built within a period of
around ten years with extraordinary
speed. Kuwait is a city that has broken
many records in hasty and speedy
buildup and buildup with haste and
speed. The sciences of planning, priority
organization, programming and phasing
must have fallen victim to the formula
of speed. Genesis tells us the world
was created in seven days.
'Let there be …' and there was.
In Kuwait a fantastic urban complex
was built, predominantly, within
the past ten years.

SABA GEORGE SHIBER
The Kuwait Urbanization
1964[1]

The Gulf Urbanisation

Astonishing for both its scope and depth of
thought, Saba George Shiber's *The Kuwait
Urbanization* documents the transformation
of the Gulf city by an astute architect-planner
who provided a cogent critique while
working to guide development from within.
Equally astonishing is the fact that one
could retrospectively substitute the name of
numerous other Gulf cities for 'Kuwait' in the
passage and it would remain accurate.

JORDAN

IRAQ

KUWAIT

BAHRAIN

SAUDI ARABIA

YEMEN

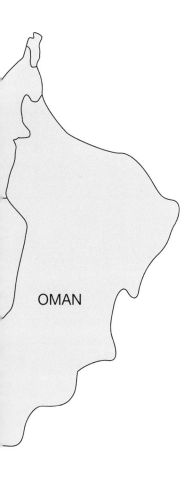

OMAN

Halloum,
f the Gulf
ration Council
countries,

untries comprising
are Bahrain,
Oman, Qatar,
rabia and the
Arab Emirates.

cp. clients

Certainly <u>speed</u> has impacted contemporary architecture and urbanism in the United Arab Emirates (UAE) and in the neighbouring countries comprising the Gulf Cooperation Council (GCC). The pace of development not only transformed the physical dimensions of cities, but also resulted in demographic imbalances, changes in legal structures and, perhaps most significantly, challenges to preconceptions about the 'Middle East'. The rapid expansion of cities in the Gulf prior to the global financial crisis in late 2008 supported ambitious aspirations to transform the region. Following a prolonged period of restructuring state-run developers and re-evaluating state-sponsored development, construction activity has steadily increased and at least some of the projects delayed by financial exigency are moving forward. This once again raises critical and complex questions related to the design of the built environment.

The expansion of cities like Dubai and Doha results in global media attention that focuses on the scale and speed of growth; however, <u>characterisations are often reduced to caricature</u>, which prohibits a more nuanced <u>understanding of the</u> forces that shape architecture and urbanism in the region.[2] Such criticism tended towards oversimplification and often failed to acknowledge the challenges associated with modern state formation in a complex region. Of course Gulf cities share many commonalities with counterparts around the world. For example, the desire for differentiation to attract foreign direct investment, multinational business and tourism is evident in ever-higher high-rises, new urban districts, artificial islands and strategically located free zones, as well as cultural and educational institutions that have built their 'brand' elsewhere.

While cities around the globe struggle to remain fiscally afloat, some Gulf cities benefit from substantial sovereign wealth funds to support development if revenue from oil and natural gas declines or foreign direct investment falters. State-owned investment funds ensure a degree of economic diversification and provide a future source of income. With a current value of US$773 billion, the Abu Dhabi Investment Authority is the second largest sovereign wealth fund in the world, followed by the Saudi Arabian Monetary Agency (SAMA) Foreign Holdings fund that manages US$737.6 billion in assets.[3] The Sovereign Wealth Fund Institute's rankings also place funds from Kuwait and Qatar, as well as two other UAE-based funds, in the top 20.[4] In addition to providing an indication of the wealth concentrated in the GCC, the investment strategies of sovereign wealth funds highlight the connection to global flows of capital and the interdependence between Gulf countries and other nations.

Model of Lusail City,
Doha, Qatar,
2007

Model of Lusail City on display at the Cityscape Global real-estate investment trade show in Dubai. Planned to cover 38 square kilometres (15 square miles), the projected population will be 450,000 people. The model, and others like it, were used to attract off-plan buyers prior to the economic downturn that impacted real-estate sales in the Gulf in late 2008.

Population of Major
Cities in the GCC,
2014

Graph showing the population (in millions) of the largest cities in the GCC. (Data source: www.arabianbusiness.com/photos/population-melting-pot-expats-v-locals-across-gulf-555330.html).

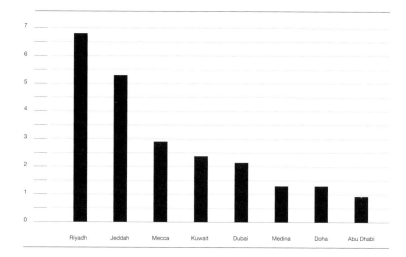

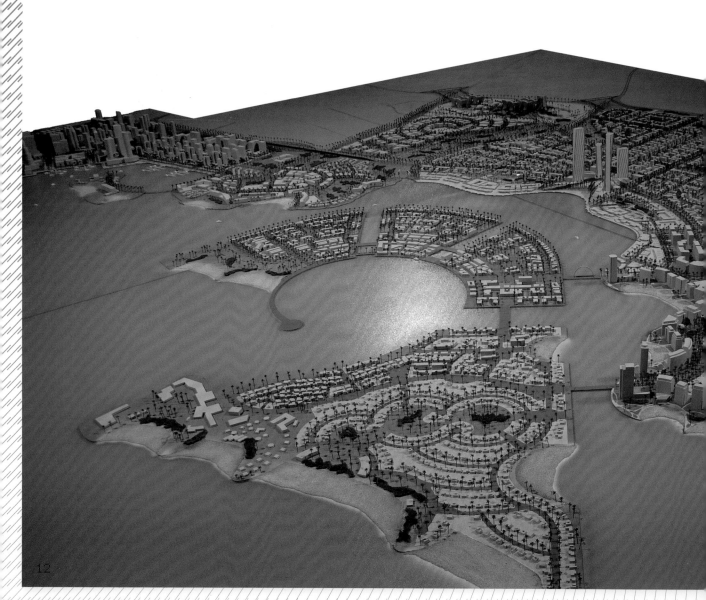

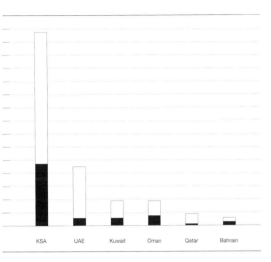

KSA   UAE   Kuwait   Oman   Qatar   Bahrain

The interdependence between the GCC, the region and the world at large has been vital for supporting the growth of Gulf cities for centuries. As Lawrence Potter notes:

> The Gulf has always been a key international trade route connecting the Middle East to India, East Africa, Southeast Asia, and China. Its orientation was outward, toward the Indian Ocean, and its society reflected this. A cosmopolitan, mercantile, and tolerant society developed here, which thrived in spite of the lack of local resources. The mobility of these people and their assets differed markedly from that of the oasis-based agricultural peasant societies that arose in the interior of neighboring states.[5]

Dubai capitalised on its prime location on a trade route and took deliberate measures such as creating favourable conditions for merchants to relocate from the Persian coast in the 1920s, improving port facilities along the creek in the 1950s, and developing the port at Jebel Ali in the 1970s. The facilities at Jebel Ali remain the largest in the Middle East and, according to a report in 2013, the recently established Abu Dhabi-based Khalifa Port 'intends to become a global mega port. It and the Kizad zone are forecast to create more than 100,000 jobs and contribute 15 per cent of Abu Dhabi's non-oil GDP by 2030, when capacity is expected to reach 15 million TEUs, which equals the current capacity of Jebel Ali port.'[6]

The creation of jobs through economic diversification initiatives such as large-scale port projects will contribute to accelerating urbanisation and will exacerbate present and future challenges associated with building and maintaining cities in the Gulf. While GCC citizens will benefit from job creation in the private sector, there will likely be continued reliance on an expatriate labour force to support economic growth. Despite the uncertainty associated with the lack of permanent residency and other challenges, 'push' factors such as unemployment and unsettled situations in the broader region and 'pull' factors such as job opportunities and the promise of higher wages than those available in the home country sustain labour migration. This of course results in imbalances between citizen and expatriate populations. In terms of demographic distribution, there is significant variation across the Gulf: estimates indicate that Bahrain has the highest citizen:expatriate ratio (49 per cent of the population are citizens), while expatriates in the UAE are estimated to constitute 87 per cent of the total population.[7] Projections forecast that the total population in the UAE will increase from approximately 9 million in 2014 to 11.5 million in 2017; if this prediction proves to be accurate, then the overall percentage of expatriates will further increase.

A survey of contemporary approaches to urban form
and the appearance of buildings throughout
the Gulf reveals widely divergent viewpoints regarding
what may be appropriate for the context at the beginning
of the 21st century.

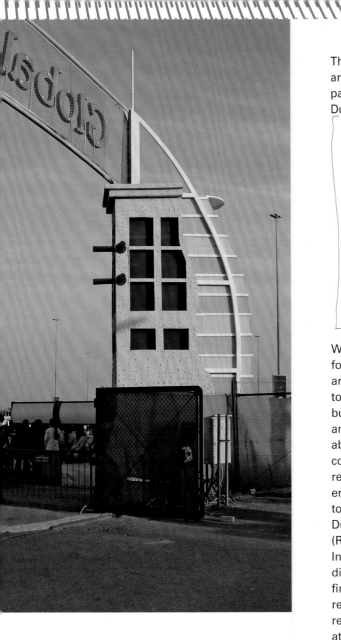

Entry to Global Village,
Dubai, UAE,
2008

The folly that defined the entry to Dubai's
Global Village, a collection of pavilions
representing different nations, aptly
captures the struggle between adapting
the past and adopting iconic expressions
in the present.

The challenges that demographic trends present for
architects and planners are addressed in the following
passage from an essay entitled 'In What Style Should
Dubai Build?':

> Should architecture in Dubai respond to the citizens
> who form part of a shrinking minority or to the
> expatriate population comprising the majority? And,
> if it is to be the expatriates, which group(s) should
> be privileged? The apolitical response would be to
> answer that architecture should respond to and serve
> all, which presupposes universalizing tendencies
> that deny the cultural differences present within the
> heterogeneous population that has enriched, and
> made substantial contributions to growth in, the Gulf.
> And the unease manifested through concerns about
> identity reveals that the negation of difference would
> certainly prove problematic.'[8]

While some non-citizen families have been in the Gulf
for multiple generations, many living in major GCC cities
are transient. There are fundamental questions related
to belonging, rights and responsibilities that impact the
built environment. Despite efforts to increase oversight
and monitoring, continuing concerns have been voiced
about labour-related policies for those working in the
construction industry. There are also unresolved issues
related to real-estate ownership as some buyers were
enticed by promises of long-term residency. In response
to problems associated with an unregulated market,
Dubai established the Real Estate Regulatory Agency
(RERA) in 2007 to provide a legislative framework.
In 2013, a legal committee was established to settle
disputes related to projects cancelled after the global
financial crisis. In this respect, Dubai has led the Gulf
region by taking steps to address some of the issues
related to the speculation that drove rapid urbanisation
at the turn of the 20th century.

Developing legislation governing the property rights
of the expatriate population in the GCC is tied to
broader questions about identity, and these questions
are extremely relevant to architecture and urbanism.
A survey of contemporary approaches to urban form
and the appearance of buildings throughout the Gulf
reveals widely divergent viewpoints regarding what may
be appropriate for the context at the beginning of the
21st century. These range from references to imagined
pasts in projects such as Madinat Jumeirah resort (2004)
in Dubai to the minimalism that characterises Saudi
Arabia's Princess Nora Bint Abdulrahman University
Health Sciences Campus (2011) designed by Perkins+Will/
Dar Al-Handasah (Shair and Partners). Beyond stylistic
concerns there are fundamental questions related to
how architecture and urbanism respond to socio-cultural
factors, such as the demand for distinguishing public
and private space at the domestic scale and the changing
nature of social relations brought about as compact
urban settlements have been abandoned in favour of
sprawling suburbs.

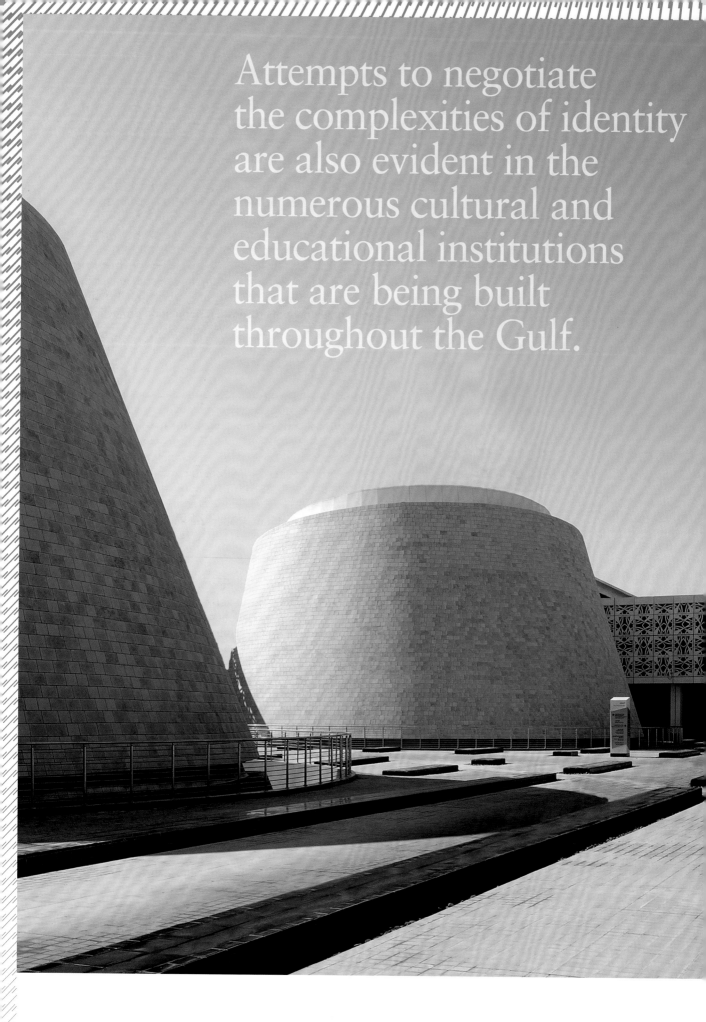

Attempts to negotiate the complexities of identity are also evident in the numerous cultural and educational institutions that are being built throughout the Gulf.

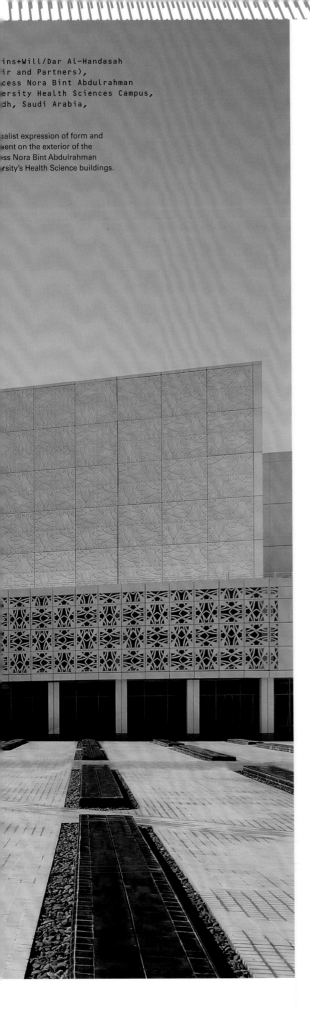

ins+Will/Dar Al-Handasah
ir and Partners),
cess Nora Bint Abdulrahman
ersity Health Sciences Campus,
dh, Saudi Arabia,

alist expression of form and
ent on the exterior of the
ss Nora Bint Abdulrahman
rsity's Health Science buildings.

Attempts to negotiate the complexities of identity are also evident in the numerous cultural and educational institutions that are being built throughout the Gulf. The models for these enterprises are as varied as the works of architecture designed for them, from the importation of 'branches' of institutions that have homes elsewhere to indigenous organisations that have been established with the explicit aim of serving the needs of the region. Prominent examples of the former include the US-based universities that have established branch campuses in Qatar's Education City and museums for Abu Dhabi's Saadiyat Cultural District, including the Louvre Abu Dhabi (2015) and the Guggenheim Abu Dhabi (due for completion in 2017). In contrast, Bahrain, Saudi Arabia and the emirate of Sharjah have focused on the development of institutions that are developed from within. As mentioned above, if population projections are correct then increases will impact the percentage of citizens relative to expatriates, and the debates regarding identity may intensify.

Projected population increases will also continue to strain resources. Supplying water and electricity to and disposing of waste produced by expanding urban populations in the GCC presents significant challenges. A report entitled *The GCC in 2020: Resources for the Future* concluded that energy consumption per head (in kilogrammes of oil equivalent) in the GCC was slightly below the US in 2005 and, by 2010, consumption in the GCC was estimated to far exceed it.[9] The report also predicted significant increases in the consumption of water across the region, highlighting that demand in Dubai could increase from 41,354 million imperial gallons in 2000 to an estimated 155,109 million imperial gallons in 2020.[10] These figures provide some indication of the stress on the environment that results from urbanisation processes in the Gulf.

Initiatives such as the UAE's Masdar Institute (2010) and the King Abdullah University of Science and Technology (KAUST) (2009), located in Saudi Arabia, are focused on research related to sustainability. These initiatives may have long-term benefits for the region, but there are pressing environmental concerns associated with an expanding population in a water-scarce region. To alleviate some of the more immediate challenges, some countries have integrated principles of sustainability into existing building regulations or have developed new standards. However, as with all regulations and standards, success will depend upon consistency in terms of compliance and enforcement. Also, as analysts have pointed out, the fact that the cost of water and electricity remain low as a result of continuing dependence on subsidies can hinder efforts to implement and enforce sustainability-related measures.

HOK,
King Abdullah University
of Science and
Technology (KAUST),
Thuwal, Saudi Arabia,
2009

Rendered view of the KAUST campus
and analysis of the climate-related
factors that impacted the design of
the buildings.

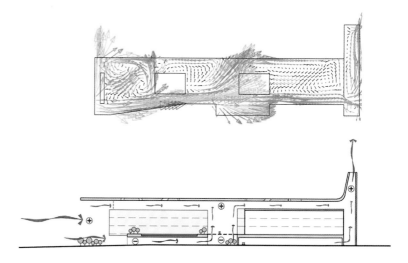

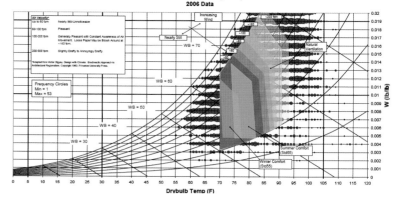

Campus aerial rendering.

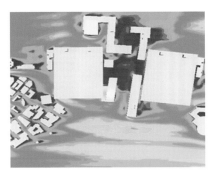

Psychrometric chart with CFD
study and wind model.

In order to provide a more nuanced understanding of how architecture and urbanism have shaped cities in the GCC, this issue of 𝔻 examines notable projects and considers how they can be understood in relation to the aspirations and demands of a region experiencing rapid growth and significant transformation. The issue focuses on specific aspects of development that have historically influenced Gulf cities, as well as highlighting emerging trends that undoubtedly impact the future of the built environment in the GCC. Topics include culture and education, urban plans and architectural typologies, and sustainable initiatives. By addressing the complex role of architecture and urbanism in the making of Gulf cities, we attempt to provide insight into the present. Taking Shiber's *The Kuwait Urbanization* as a model, the issue seeks to provide an overview of contemporary development that favours critique over caricature. 𝔻

Notes
1. Saba George Shiber, *The Kuwait Urbanization*, Kuwait Government Printing Office (Kuwait), 1964, p 151.
2. For a discussion of architecture and urbanism in Dubai during the intense period of development prior to 2008, see Kevin Mitchell, 'The Future Promise of Architecture in Dubai', in Ahmed Kanna (ed), *The Superlative City: Dubai and the Urban Condition in the Early Twenty-First Century*, Harvard University Graduate School of Design/Harvard University Press (Cambridge, MA), 2013, pp 148–66.
3. www.swfinstitute.org/fund-rankings/.
4. *Ibid.*
5. Lawrence Potter, 'Introduction', in Lawrence Potter (ed), *The Persian Gulf in History*, Palgrave Macmillan (New York), 2009, p 1.
6. Dania Saadi, 'UAE's Khalifa Port and Jebel Ali Lead Way in Port Developments', *The National*, 24 October 2013: www.thenational.ae/business/industry-insights/shipping/uaes-khalifa-port-and-jebel-ali-lead-way-in-port-developments.
7. www.arabianbusiness.com/photos/population-melting-pot-expats-v-locals-across-gulf-555330.html.
8. Kevin Mitchell, 'In What Style Should Dubai Build?', in Elisabeth Blum and Peter Neitzke (eds), *Dubai: City from Nothing*, Birkhäuser (Basel), 2009, p 138.
9. The Economist Intelligence Unit, *The GCC in 2020: Resources for the Future*, The Economist Intelligence Unit Limited, 2010, p 6: http://graphics.eiu.com/upload/eb/GCC_in_2020_Resources_WEB.pdf.
10. *Ibid*, p 13.

Sarina Wakefield

m

oment

Gulf

Architecture

How might interpretations of the past be informing the culture of tomorrow? **Sarina Wakefield,** a specialist in heritage and museum development in the Middle East, provides an overview of the form and function of contemporary museums in Qatar, Bahrain, Saudi Arabia and the UAE. In so doing, she explores how institutions are drawing on locally specific heritage and cultural objects to develop distinctive identities for an international audience.

Tadao Ando,
Maritime Museum,
Saadiyat Marina
District,
Saadiyat Island
Abu Dhabi, UAE,
ongoing

previous spread: Artist's impression of the proposed museum illustrating how the clean lines of the building merge with the surrounding seascape.

Ateliers Jean Nouvel,
National Museum
of Qatar,
Doha, Qatar,
due for completion
2016

The design for the National Museum makes reference to Qatar's natural environment through disc-shaped planes that appear to rise from the site like a desert rose.

Museums have been present in the Gulf since the 1950s,[1] and since 2000 there has been a proliferation of state-led large-scale 'iconic' projects, many of which are still under construction. Like their counterparts in Asia and the West, museum projects in the Gulf are not immune to the desire for iconic buildings by invited internationally recognised architects. Many of these developments have been highly criticised for trying to replicate Western-style museums and for 'importing culture'. However, by analysing the architectural form and the function of some of these new museums, in particular those in Qatar, Bahrain, Saudi Arabia and the UAE, it is possible to see how different aspects of the past are being employed to develop distinctive identities using locally derived themes to address a global audience.

Qatar Museums: Nation and Identity

The Qatar Museums Authority (QMA) was formed in 2005 with the aim of developing Qatar into a regional cultural centre. This was a measured move by the government whose directive is to reinforce and promote Qatari national identity locally, regionally and internationally. QMA's vision focuses on the development of national museums and the preservation of cultural heritage.[2] The most visible manifestations are Qatar's flagship museum projects: the National Museum of Qatar and the Museum of Islamic Art.

The development of the National Museum of Qatar marks a measured move by the Qatari government to use architecture to establish its identity. Qatar's original National Museum opened in 1975 in a restored palace built in the early 20th century by Sheikh Abdullah bin Jassim Al-Thani. This early museum served as his family residence and the seat of government for 25 years.[3] In 1980 the building won the Aga Khan Award for restoration and rehabilitation of Islamic architecture. Although not currently operational, redevelopment plans draw on the theme of Qatar's natural history and environment for inspiration.

Jean Nouvel's design for the National Museum, located on a prominent site in Doha and scheduled for completion in 2016, draws inspiration from the desert re 'a mineral formation of crystallized sand found in the briny layer just beneath the desert's surface'.[4] A building information modelling (BIM) project was developed b Gehry Technologies to ensure the accura and workability of the complex design, which consisted of 'tilting, interpenetrati disks that define the pavilion's floors, wa and roofs'[5] and seeks to establish an ico image for the museum. Nouvel's design links the inside and outside of the museu by incorporating a 110,000-square-metre (1.2-million-square-foot) landscaped park Influenced by the local environment, the park will become a 'Qatari desert landsca incorporating various indigenous plants. 'When complete the museum will house 8,000 square metres (86,000 square feet) permanent gallery space, which will featu three central themes: the natural history the Qatar peninsula, the social and cultur history of Qatar, and the history of Qatar as a nation from the 18th century to the present.'[6]

Qatar's ambitions to become a cultur centre have also focused on Islamic cultu and identity through the development of the Museum of Islamic Art, which opened in 2008. Designed by IM Pei, the 35,000-square-metre (377,000-square-foo museum aims to be 'the foremost museu of Islamic art in the world'.[7] It is inspired b the domed ablution fountain at the Ibn Tu Mosque in Cairo, and used in Pei's design by layering geometric shapes to form a cubic structure.[8] The aim is to challenge misconceptions of Islam by illustrating its role as a culture, not just a religion, throu the breadth of its collection that spans 13 centuries and three continents. Through Islamic symbolism and the development of its global collections and programmes, the museum takes an overtly internationa approach.

National Museum of Saudi Arabia: an [Islam]ic Centre

[The] development of museums in Saudi [Arab]ia is related to wider policies of social [and] intellectual development. The National [Mus]eum of Saudi Arabia in Riyadh, which [open]ed in January 1999, formed part of [the g]overnment's economic development [prog]ramme to widen Saudis' economic and [cultu]ral activities. The architects, Moriyama [& Te]shima, saw the design of the museum [as an] instrument to 'help Saudis define [them]selves for the rest of the world and to [inspi]re national pride in Saudi culture and [histo]ry'.[9] The central design is a wall of local [sand]stone that forms a curved line directing [the vi]sitor's gaze towards Mecca. Inside [the 3]5,840-square-metre (385,780-square- [foot]) museum are eight major display halls [arra]nged according to historical sequence [cont]aining a collection of archaeological [find]s, documents, manuscripts, paintings and

[...] The museum's ultimate aim is to educate [visit]ors about the kingdom's history and its [relati]onship to Islam. Unlike other institutions [in th]e Gulf that have been developed for an [inter]national audience and tourists, museums [in Sa]udi Arabia face challenges due to [restr]ictive visa requirements. Therefore, the [Nati]onal Museum primarily targets regional [and] national visitors, and expatriate workers [livi]ng in Saudi. The physical building and [its co]llections are used as a space for selected [audi]ences to engage with the kingdom's past, [while] the iconic treatment of the building and [the i]nternational reputation of the architects [are u]sed to position the project globally.

IM Pei,
Museum of Islamic Art,
Doha, Qatar,
2008

IM Pei was commissioned out of retirement to design the museum, which was based on geometrical transformations found throughout the history of Arab Islamic architecture.

Moriyama & Teshima,
National Museum of Saudi Arabia,
Riyadh, Saudi Arabia,
1999

The museum's curved wall, which is strategically positioned to sweep towards Mecca, marks the entry to the building and defines an open plaza.

rkitekter,
in National Museum,
a, Bahrain,

ign for the museum draws
aini vernacular precedents to
e a functionally focused space
e and display the nation's
logical collection.

rt Arkitekter,
t al-Bahrain Site Museum,
a, Bahrain,

seum was designed to connect with
of Qal'at al-Bahrain (the Bahrain
sthetically and functionally by
ng the physical surroundings and
tor experience.

Bahrain: Architecture and the Pre-Islamic Past

The Bahrain National Museum, which is distinguished by its locally sensitive architectural design, was built in 1988 to house artefacts from extensive archaeological excavations that have contributed to knowledge of the nation's pre-Islamic past. The archaeological evidence suggests that the earliest occupation of Bahrain dates to around 5000–4000 BC, and that it became the centre of the Kingdom of Dilmun. The remains of an early Dilmun city were discovered at the site of Qal'at al-Bahrain (the Bahrain Fort).[10] Dilmun served as a trading centre from around 2500 BC, and at the height of its power it controlled Gulf trading routes. The site at Qal'at al-Bahrain would have served as an important trading stop on the routes stretching north to Mesopotamia and Assyria, south to Oman and Africa, and east to the Indus Valley.[11]

The museum was designed and developed by Bahrain-based engineers COWI Consulting in collaboration with Danish architects KHR Arkitekter. The architecture of the building is characterised by a minimalist white travertine facade, 45-degree rotations and a dramatic courtyard overlooking the seafront.[12] This is arguably due to a much greater interest in developing architecture with a local vernacular in the Middle East that was prominent in the Gulf in the 1970s and 1980s. This contrasts with the current large-scale museum projects of Qatar, Saudi Arabia and Abu Dhabi, and suggests a more contextual approach to design. In addition to the archaeological exhibits, the permanent exhibition space includes an ethnography section and a hall featuring works by some of Bahrain's leading artists. It has been 25 years since the museum opened, and to mark this milestone the Ministry of Culture has announced plans to update the museum and its collections.[13]

Rather than moving away from the earlier vernacular traditions, the new Qal'at al-Bahrain Site Museum combines these traditions with contemporary Scandinavian techniques and expertise. Opened in 2008, the 2,000-square-metre (21,500-square-foot) museum is situated to the north of the Qal'at al-Bahrain fort, which was inscribed as a UNESCO World Heritage Site in 2007.[14] Excavations around the fort have revealed residential, public, commercial and military structures that testify to the importance of the site. The museum supplements the Bahrain National Museum by displaying artefacts from the site dating from 2500 BC to the present day. It was designed and developed by Copenhagen-based Wohlert Arkitekter in collaboration with COWI Consulting. In contrast to large-scale museum projects throughout the Gulf, the Qal'at al-Bahrain Site Museum retains the 'scale of traditional buildings in Bahrain'.[15] It is designed to enhance visitors' experience of the site by providing tourist facilities and a series of pathways along the waterfront leading to the fort. Inside the museum are five halls organised around a 30-metre (100-foot) tell wall, which is representative of the fort's position atop a 17.5-hectare (43.2-acre) artificial hill (the tell). Incorporated within the tell wall is a re-creation of the site's archaeological layers that includes 500 artefacts illustrating the history of its settlement.

By drawing influence from local vernacular form and the country's archaeological past, Bahrain's museums are used to position the kingdom as a powerful centre in the region and to reinforce the importance of its continued role as a contemporary trading hub.

ther than moving away from the
lier vernacular traditions, the
v Qal'at al-Bahrain Site Museum
mbines these traditions with a
ndinavian sensibility for massing
l material.

Abu Dhabi: Architecture and Global Imagining

Abu Dhabi's global aspirations are apparent from the way in which it has chosen to work with well-known international institutions and 'starchitects' to develop iconic museums to house international collections and exhibitions. The government's strategic plan aims to develop Abu Dhabi into a global city by investing in key industry sectors and urban and cultural development.[16] In 2004, the Abu Dhabi Tourism Authority announced plans to develop Saadiyat Island into a tourist destination with the Cultural District as its centrepiece. Plans for the Cultural District include the Louvre Abu Dhabi, the Guggenheim Abu Dhabi, the Zayed National Museum and the Performing Arts Centre. The Maritime Museum will be the only museum set apart in the Saadiyat Marina District.

The Louvre Abu Dhabi is the result of a bilateral agreement between the UAE and France that solidifies the cultural relations between the two nations. The 24,000-square-metre (258,300-square-foot) museum is being developed with the expertise of both the Musée du Louvre and Agence France-Muséums, and is expected to open in December 2015. The design is representative of a 'museum city', referencing how architect Jean Nouvel has positioned the collection of buildings, ponds and landscaping in a similar way to that of an ancient city.[17] The 180-metre (590-foot) geometric lace dome is inspired by the interlaced palm leaves traditionally used as roofing material that will allow light to filter into the museum.

The Guggenheim Abu Dhabi is being developed in collaboration with the Solomon R Guggenheim Foundation and is expected to open in 2017. Designed by architect Frank Gehry, it is set to be the largest museum in the Cultural District, containing 13,000 square metres (140,000 square feet) of gallery space in what is described as a 'monumental pile of gallery boxes'.[18] Eleven cone-like structures will provide a further 18,000 square metres (194,000 square feet) of exhibition space. Gehry drew his inspiration from the region's ancient wind towers that both ventilate and shade the museum's exterior courtyards.

Museum branding is a key element within the development of both the Louvre Abu Dhabi and the Guggenheim Abu Dhabi. However, the balancing of local and franchised heritage is an important issue and one that is partly addressed by incorporating local elements within the architectural design that are used as iconic features to promote the projects to global audiences.

Foster + Partners,
Zayed National Museum,
Saadiyat Cultural District,
Saadiyat Island,
Abu Dhabi, UAE,
due for completion 2016

Rendering showing the wing-like towers, which are intended to make a visual reference to the traditional practice of falconry within the UAE.

Frank Gehry,
Guggenheim Abu Dhabi,
Saadiyat Cultural District,
Saadiyat Island,
Abu Dhabi, UAE,
due for completion 2017

Rendering of the proposed museum illustrating the arrangement of individual masses that contain the gallery spaces.

The Zayed National Museum will for centrepiece of the Cultural District, focus on the life of Sheikh Zayed bin Sultan al Nahyan, ruler of Abu Dhabi and Presiden of the UAE from its founding in 1971 to h death in 2004.[19] Designed by Foster + Par and developed in consultation with the B Museum, the Zayed National Museum is scheduled to open in 2016. It will house s permanent galleries exploring the histor heritage and culture of the UAE. One of t central themes is falconry, which is reflec in both the symbolism of the architecture the content. Five towers, made of lightw steel, resemble the wings of a falcon risi from a constructed mound. The museum also maintain falconry traditions by inclu a falcon conservation centre.[20]

The Maritime Museum will be built o shoreline of Saadiyat Island's Marina Dis Designed by Tadao Ando, the architectur provides a symbolic link between the sea and the land. Its rectangular box shape features a central arch, cut diagonally by hyperbolic paraboloid curve[21] framing a (traditional regional sailing boat) floating the water beneath the building. Although few details have been released, the focus on the UAE's seafaring history[22] illustrate along with the Zayed National Museum's inclusion of falconry, the way in which th national museums are using traditional a intangible aspects of the UAE's past with the construction of global architectural fc

The discourse that surrounds the museums in Abu Dhabi suggests that the aim is not just to create museums, but ic through the use of internationally renow architects and global museum brands. Th approach reflects the UAE's continuing efforts to negotiate its transnational and cosmopolitan identity.

Museums as Agents of Identity-Making in the Gulf

This brief discussion of selected museum projects in the Gulf illustrates how the architecture of museums, their emphasis as reflected in the collections, and their management are being consciously developed by the Gulf states to assert distinct national identities and roles within the region. In Qatar, museum architecture and collections present the nation's history and Islamic roots as key aspects of its contemporary identity, with the aim of establishing the country as a major cultural player in the region. For Saudi Arabia, museum development is being used to reinforce its importance within the Islamic world. Although developed for national and regional tourists interested in the cultural heritage of Saudi Arabia, the global architecture transcends national boundaries and region-specific references. In Bahrain, museums have been used to showcase the nation's cultural heritage since the opening of the Bahrain National Museum in 1988. More recently there has been a conscious shift towards using the existing National Museum and the new Qal'at al-Bahrain Site Museum to convey the country's historical importance. Although its economic and political role has been established for some time, Abu Dhabi is now positioning itself as a global centre by constructing a cosmopolitan identity through museum architecture and collections that are transnational in scope. In sum, contemporary approaches to museum development in the Gulf reflect attempts to negotiate national, regional and international identities, and the buildings designed by architects from across the world reveal aspirations for global recognition. ⚮

Notes

1. One of the earliest known museums is the Kuwait Museum which opened in 1957 and closed in 1983. In Qatar, the National Museum of Qatar opened in 1975 (in 2004 it closed for refurbishment). In Bahrain, the Bahrain National Museum opened in 1988. In the UAE, the Al-Ain Museum opened in 1969 in Abu Dhabi, the Dubai Museum in 1971, and the Fujairah Museum in 1970. In Saudi Arabia, the Museum of Archaeology and Ethnography opened in 1978 and later closed in 1999. Finally the Oman Museum opened in 1974.
2. Qatar Museums: www.qm.org.qa/en.
3. *Ibid.*
4. Gehry Technologies, National Museum of Qatar Project Summary: www.gehrytechnologies.com/sites/default/files/images/National-Museum-of-Qatar.pdf.
5. *Ibid.*
6. www.qma.com.qa/en/collections/national-museum-of-qatar.
7. www.mia.org.qa/en/about/the-museum-building.
8. 'National Museum of Qatar by Jean Nouvel', *Dezeen*, 24 March 2010: www.dezeen.com/2010/03/24/national-museum-of-qatar-by-jean-nouvel/.
9. Moriyama & Teshima Architects, 'The National Museum Saudi Arabia: A Case Study': www.mtarch.com/mtasanmcasestudy.html.
10. Geoffrey Bibby, *Looking for Dilmun*, Stacey International (London), 1996.
11. Rachel MacLean and Timothy Insoll, *An Archaeological Guide to Bahrain*, Archeopress (Oxford), 2011.
12. Ministry of Culture, Bahrain National Museum: http://www.moc.gov.bh/en/VisitingBahrain/Destinations/BahrainNationalMuseum/.
13. Sylvia Smith, 'Bahrain National Museum Expands Horizons', BBC News, 23 January 2014: www.bbc.com/news/world-middle-east-25733814.
14. Wohlert Arkitekter, Qal'at al-Bahrain: www.wohlertarkitekter.com/qalat-al-bahrain/.
15. Ministry of Culture, Qal'at al-Bahrain site and museum: www.moc.gov.bh/en/top10/Name,7518,en.html.
16. Abu Dhabi Urban Planning Council, 'Capital 2030', Plan Abu Dhabi 2030: Urban Structure Framework Plan, 2007: http://www.upc.gov.ae/abu-dhabi-2030/capital-2030.aspx?lang=en-US.
17. Tourism Development Investment Corporation, 'Outside the Museum': www.saadiyat.ae/en/cultural/louvre-abu-dhabi1/louvre-abu-dhabi-architecture-outside.html.
18. Tourism Development Investment Corporation, 'Inside the Museum': www.saadiyat.ae/en/cultural/guggenheim-abu-dhabi1/architecture2.html.
19. Tourism Development Investment Corporation 'Overview': www.saadiyat.ae/en/cultural/zayed-national-museum/znm-overview.html.
20. See also Sarina Wakefield, 'Falconry as Heritage in the United Arab Emirates', *World Archaeology*, 44(2), 2012, pp 280–90.
21. Emmanuel Petit, 'The Gate of Creation: Tadao Ando's Design School in Mexico', *Architectural Review*, 4 November 2013: www.architectural-review.com/buildings/the-gate-of-creation-tadao-andos-design-school-in-mexico/8654552.article.
22. Tourism Development Investment Corporation, 'Inside the Museum', *op cit*.

ers Jean Nouvel,
e Abu Dhabi,
yat Cultural District,
yat Island,
habi, UAE,

ing of the proposed museum
g how the domed roof filters
rough patterned surfaces that
eference to traditional Arabian
cture.

Mona El Mousfy and Sharmeen Syed

Cultural Exchange and Urban Appropriation

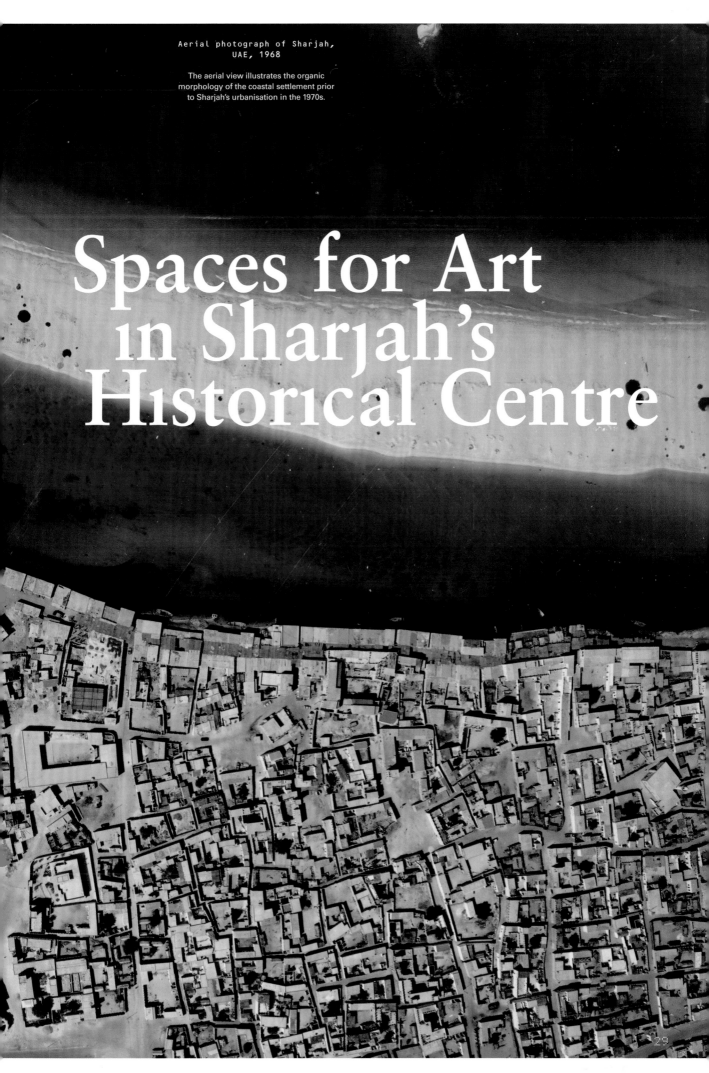

Aerial photograph of Sharjah,
UAE, 1968

The aerial view illustrates the organic
morphology of the coastal settlement prior
to Sharjah's urbanisation in the 1970s.

Spaces for Art in Sharjah's Historical Centre

There is a common misconception that culture in the Gulf must be entirely newly imported and artificial. Architect **Mona El Mousfy** and architect and researcher **Sharmeen Syed,** who have both been engaged as architects for the Sharjah Art Foundation Art Spaces project and the Sharjah Biennial, challenge the notion of 'constructed heritage' at Sharjah in UAE. They show Sharjah to be a highly adaptive, historically multiethnic city that is characterised by its cultural fluidity.

Since the 16th century, Sharjah has been identified as a crucial and strategically significa port in the UAE region given its position on major sea trade routes. It consequently developed into a trade hub and city of cultura exchange. The city's formation in the early 20th century demonstrates an inherent social openness and urban fluidity. The histories of spaces for exhibition in the city and the transformative relation between art, culture ar urban form challenge the initial urban reading that constructed heritage represents the city's only cultural identity. The idealised and insula cultural narrative along with constructed herit have in fact obscured a complex and fluid soci urban history of the city's nucleus defined by coastal settlement traces.

The urban premise of the city of Sharjah was a [me]rcantile settlement. Until the 1970s, the coast [was] predominantly occupied by the souk, which [too]k on the linear and continuous characteristic [of t]he shoreline. Shops had a direct relation with [the] water and were built with the specific function [of r]eceiving and loading goods from and on to [dho]ws along the creek's shore on one end and [sup]plying them on the storefront along the interior [alle]y of the souk at the other. As the main site [of e]conomic subsistence and cultural exchange, [the] souk had the most anchored presence on [the] urban scale, stretching approximately a [kilo]metre between Al Mareijah and Al Mujarrah. [An] uninterrupted segment ran along the Al [Sha]waihean area: Souk Saqr or the Iranian Souk [refe]rring to the majority of Iranian merchants.

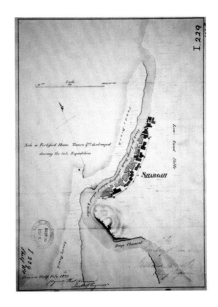

Historical map of Sharjah,
1820

The figure-ground map is the first recorded
delineation of the coastal settlement of Sharjah.

Sharjah Creek,
1926

Up until the 1960s, Sharjah had a direct relation
to the water with the coastline acting as an
interface between accosted boats and the souk.

Coastal Settlement as a Ground for Exchange

Merchants were key actors in the formation of the fluid urban character of Gulf coastal cities. In Sharjah they settled along the creek in the two central neighbourhoods, Al Shuwaihean to the northeast and Al Mareijah to the southwest.[1] Pearl trade was the main industry of Gulf coastal settlements between the 18th and early 20th centuries. Merchants' houses with valued architectural character played a key role in Sharjah's architectural history. In the 1990s, as a response to spatial needs, they were appropriated to serve in new capacities such as exhibition spaces, art galleries and artist studios, with no claim of explicit transgression of the literal gallery space, nor the reconceptualisation of the museum space.[2]

Until the 1960s, the majority of the population consisted of impoverished pearl divers and fishermen living in Arish (palm) huts, and some upgraded to rudimentary coral masonry houses. Pearl merchants' houses were large estates in proximity to the souk and relatively more permanent by virtue of materiality. A few of these houses survived the rapid post-oil urbanisation, deterioration and decay due to abandonment and/or neglect, to eventually be cited for their historical and architectural merit. Architectural typologies, elements and decorative treatments such as tiles and carving patterns were often imported or brought back on travels, notably from Iran and India, by merchants.[3] Bait Al Naboodah is the most characteristic of an affluent pearl merchant's residence. Located near Souk Al Arsa in Al Mareijah, it was built in the early 20th century by Isa Bin Obaid Al Naboodah, a prominent pearl merchant. Its highly decorative, ready-carved wooden teak columns of iconic style were imported from India, and delicately defined the loggia space on the ground floor (later added to the first floor) around the north and east sides of the courtyard. Another comparable merchant's house is Bait Al Shamsi, located at the northeast end of the Iranian Souk in

Al Shuwaihean. Prior to the 1990s renovation the house engaged with the souk with a creek entrance adjacent to the shops. Of particular interest is the room on the roof towards the creek: its five long windows crested with equally wide panels are decorated with charcoal-stained floral motifs of Iranian origin.

Adjacent to the Iranian Souk is Bait Al Serkal, which belonged to Issa bin Abdul Latif Al Serkal, a British native agent for the Arabian Gulf, embodying a different history of Sharjah. It comprises three sets of stairs and 24 rooms over three storeys, attesting to the influential role of its owner. Its square-shaped courtyard is surrounded by loggias on two floors. It features blank facades on the ground floor, stained-glass windows on its first floor, and a

*Merchants were key
actors in the formation of
the fluid urban character
of Gulf coastal cities.*

corner terrace on the third floor. Bait Al Serkal became the property of Sheikh Muhammad bin Saqr Al Qasimi in 1951, signifying the end of one form of the British presence, and was converted into a maternity hospital run by nuns. The descendants of the owners of the Bait Al Naboodah and Bait Al Shamsi houses occupied them up until the 1970s when they abandoned them for modern houses in the city's new suburbs after the oil boom initiated fully-fledged urbanisation and a distributive economy.

Since the early 1990s, Bait Al Naboodah has housed a permanent 'heritage' installation that is primarily intended to sensitise young Emiratis to the life of their ancestors. Bait Al Serkal and Bait Al Shamsi were programmed as artist studios, and an art exhibition space, respectively. Between 1995 and 1997, prior to the construction of the Sharjah Art Museum, Bait Al Serkal was designated as the Sharjah Art Institute. These buildings were programmed as cultural spaces after being selected for restoration based on architectural and historical values as a result of an emerging discourse on preservation in the late 1980s. However, reconstruction of Sharjah's historical centre in the 1990s did not follow a grand integrated scheme. The area behind the Iranian Souk, where the Shamsi and the Serkal houses are located, presents a good example of urban and social transformations over the span of three decades. In the early 1990s the neighbourhood was very densely populated; however, inhabitants were gradually evicted and small and decrepit traditional courtyard and palm houses were removed to clear the area for the construction of the first Sharjah Art Museum and partial reconstruction of surrounding historical houses. The long and imposing two-storey modern museum building overlooks the newly created Arts Square towards the Iranian Souk. Islamic and regional decorative features, such as arched stained-glass windows, perforated decorative panels and symbolic wind towers flanking central entry doors, modify the Modernist architectural expression in an attempt to relate to the surrounding historical buildings.

Another notable building from the pre-1960s layer was the residence of the British Political Agent in Sharjah, located on the coast in Al Mujarrah. The building was demolished to allow for the development of the site into the Souk Al Mujarrah in 1987. At the time there was a resolute effort to erase colonial links regardless of architectural or historical importance. The house was a revered example of an expansive courtyard typology, and upon the closing of the British agency, it was converted into the Seaface Hotel. The new imposing building of the Souk Al Mujarrah was indicative of the advent of a new architectural typology in Sharjah – massive, linear blocks ornamented with references to 'Islamic' architecture.

The late 1980s also saw a recurring wave of Islamicisation and Wahhabi influence with accelerated development of mosques and religious institutions and the ban on alcohol in 1985. The effects of conservatism took a toll on the progression of cultural programming with such voices influencing the decision-making in the cultural sector. This also proved to be a difficult time for non-traditional visual artists to build an audience

Extension of Non-Museum Spaces for Art

Since its formation in 1984, the Emirates Fine Arts Society prioritised audience building through publishing and programming workshops, exhibitions and ateliers. The use of non-museum spaces for exhibiting art in Sharjah was soon extended to more contemporary frontiers outside of the historical centre. The Society began to organise yearly exhibitions in the former Expo Centre Sharjah, a large tent structure that was opened in 1977 in the Al Khan area.[4] Initially intended to receive specialised trade shows, it was later also used for public events, festivals and art exhibitions. These annual exhibitions paved the way for the creation of the Sharjah Biennial in 1993. From 1993 to 2001, the Sharjah Biennial was a local and regional event and its first five editions were held in the former Expo

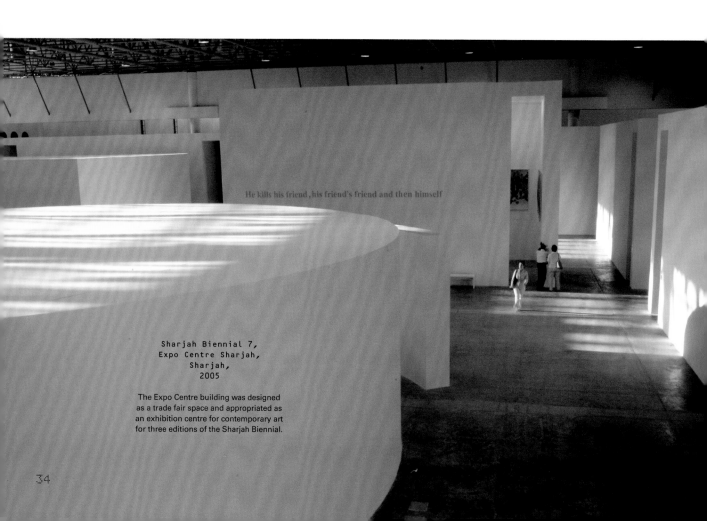

He kills his friend, his friend's friend and then himself

Sharjah Biennial 7,
Expo Centre Sharjah,
Sharjah,
2005

The Expo Centre building was designed as a trade fair space and appropriated as an exhibition centre for contemporary art for three editions of the Sharjah Biennial.

ntre. The three following editions engaged
international cultural map and marked
hift to contemporary art practices; the
esent-day Expo Centre Sharjah (which
placed the former tent structure) was the
in venue.[5]

clamation of the Historical Links
d Permeability of Art and Culture
ogrammes

reclaim historical links to the city centre,
arjah Biennial 9 relocated to the Al
uwaihean area. Following a strategy of
nsification and concentration, and to remedy
lack of exhibition spaces, artists were
couraged to occupy non-museum spaces
ch as the car park and storage facilities of
Sharjah Art Museum, as well as urban
ckets including the service road between
Museum and its annexe. As a predecessor
urban intervention, there are accounts
early and experimental art performances
conceptual artist Hassan Sharif in urban
es of Al Mareijah. This was also the
ighbourhood where the first art atelier was
ablished by the Emirates Fine Arts Society.[6]
With the formation of the Sharjah Art
undation, an institution that emerged from
Sharjah Biennial and its broader range
cultural programming, the necessity to
vision new fluid exhibition spaces anchored
Sharjah's historical area became evident.
is need led to an ambitious urban adaptive
use project in Al Mareijah. The Sharjah Art
undation Art Spaces project consisted of
e buildings conceived as exhibition spaces
contemporary art. The aim was to retain
place's historical footprint, reinterpret
e-existing or documented architectural
ces within the plot, and readapt historical
chitectural elements and materiality to new
es and conditions. The buildings provide
ange of interiors to experience art with a
riety of exterior spaces including courtyards,
eyways, open squares and an interconnected
ofscape. They were first used in 2013 for
arjah Biennial 11. This was also the first

Maider Lopez,
Football Field,
Arts Square,
Al Shuwaihean, Sharjah,
2009

The photograph includes a frontal view of the Sharjah Art
Museum and shows the Arts Square occupied by Maider
Lopez's urban installation.

Sheela Gowda,
Drip Field,
Sharjah Biennial 9,
Bait Al Serkal, Sharjah,
2009

A service road between the Sharjah Art Museum
and its annexe was occupied for an urban installation
during Sharjah Biennial 9.

Gitah Meh,
Soffreh,
Sharjah Biennial 9,
Bait Al Serkal, Sharjah,
2009

The occupation of a courtyard space for an art
installation. A glimpse of Sharjah Creek can also be
seen in the background.

time there was an attempt to create a spatial fluidity across Bank Street, a thoroughfare dating from the urban masterplan executed in the 1970s that physically divided the continuity between the Al Mareijah and Al Shuwaihean neighbourhoods and ruptured the vital continuity of the souk at the time.

Urban Potentialities

The Bank Street fragment is formed of mid-rise buildings aligned on either side of a 70-metre (230-foot) wide thoroughfare and the reconstructed Al Hisn fort located at its centre. It is the encapsulation of a specific wave of urban and architectural modernity in Sharjah, and an era when there was a clear impetus towards economic development resulting in drastic changes in the physical form and social realm of the city. Responding to a spatial need, a building along Bank Street was occupied during Sharjah Biennial 11, extending the use of non-museum spaces to yet another building type. The Sharjah Islamic Bank building is scheduled for demolition in order to reconstruct the ruler's house, which once stood on the site. The building was

Superflex,
The Bank,
Sharjah Biennial 11,
Bank Street, Sharjah,
2014

An urban intervention by artists' collective Superflex temporarily reclaimed an urban island along the centre of Bank Street for Sharjah Biennial 11.

Sharjah Art Foundation
Art Spaces,
Al Mareijah, Sharjah,
2013

Bird's-eye view of the Foundation's
Art Spaces (centre) inscribed within
an existing layer of historic and
renovated urban fabric.

partially gutted and used as a temporary venue for the biennial.

For the same biennial, Superflex, a Danish artists' collective, envisioned a site-specific urban installation that occupies a temporary reclaimed urban island. The collective imagined a new, non-monetary banking model that converted memories into physical urban objects that inhabitants from the area were asked to nominate from their countries of origin. These objects were then reproduced and placed in a temporary urban park: *The Bank*. The project mended, physically and socially, this extended urban space and demonstrated social activation through the turnout of hundreds of people who occupied the park as users.

Sharjah's cultural production and spaces for art can be seen as bringing ambiguous and contradictory experiences. Nevertheless, the patterns of spatial, programmatic and urban shifts in relation to its cultural activities reveal a fluid occupation of museum and non-museum spaces rather than a prescriptive meta-approach to institutional presence. Spaces as varied as merchant houses, commercial trade buildings, modern mid-rises and urban pockets have been appropriated for durations spanning months, years or decades in a response to one-off needs and a desire to keep these spaces active. Contrary to a possible first reading, the city does not capacitate a grand scheme, but rather adapts to new shifting urban and social conditions. Sharjah's historical centre expresses a cultural fluidity of a historically multi-ethnic city – the survival of which was principally based on physical and cultural exchange. This reinforces the perspective that the vitality of the city is contingent to the preservation of its receptive and adaptive characteristics. ⌂

otes

Ayse Sema Kubat, Samia Rab, semin Ince Guney, Ozlem Ozer and rdar Kaya, 'Application of Space ntax in Developing: A Regeneration amework for Sharjah's Heritage Area', oceedings of the Eighth International ace Syntax Symposium, Santiago de ile, 2012, p 3.
Peter Osborne, 'Non-Places and e Spaces of Art', The Journal of rchitecture, 6, Summer 2001, p 188.
Robert Carter, The History and ehistory of Pearling in the Persian ulf, Koninklijke Brill NV (Leiden), 2005,

p 189.
4. Mariam Al Serkal, 'A Pioneer in Business Exhibitions, Sharjah', Gulf News, 5 September 2008.
5. Ken Lum, 'Unfolding Identities', Sharjah Biennial 7 catalogue, 2005, p 35
6. Annette Lagier, 'A Different Journey to the East: The Art of the Five from the United Arab Emirates, 5UAE' Ludwig Forum for International Arts (Aachen), 2002: http://heimat.de/5uae/ index_engl.html.

Kevin Mitchell

Design for the Future

Perkins+Will and Dar Al-Handasah
(Shair and Partners),
Princess Nora Bint Abdulrahman
University,
Riyadh, Saudi Arabia,
2011

View of the university's
internal shaded court.

Educational Institutions in the Gulf

Despite a distinguished heritage of learning in the Middle East, the expansion of provision for higher education is currently at an unprecedented scale. The Gulf States, in particular, are seeking to keep up with accelerated population growth and a demographic 'youth bulge'. Guest-Editor **Kevin Mitchell** describes the architectural approaches employed in the design of institutions in the region from the first universities in Saudi Arabia to Foster + Partners's ground-breaking sustainable design for the Masdar Institute in Abu Dhabi and future projects.

Universities and higher education institutions in the Middle East and North Africa (MENA) region are certainly not new and there is a long history of establishing centres of learning and scholarship. The University of al-Karaouine in Fez, Morocco, and Al-Azhar University in Cairo are among the oldest educational establishments in the world.[1] However, current challenges facing the region and aspirations to meet the needs of a rapidly expanding population have resulted in a substantial increase of the number of universities, with the largest expansion taking place in the Gulf Cooperation Council (GCC) countries. Since 1980 the population in the Arab region has more than doubled and, according to a study published as part of the *Arab Human Development Report Research Paper Series*, in 2010 one-third of the population was below the age of 15 and one-fifth was between 15 and 24.[2] The so-called 'youth bulge' is also evident in the GCC, with 29 per cent of the population reported to be below the age of 15 in 2008.[3]

Providing educational opportunities for youth has required government investment and the establishment of numerous public and private institutions throughout the region. A World Bank report entitled *The Road Not Traveled: Education Reform in the Middle East and Africa* showed that the region invested approximately 5 per cent of gross domestic product (GDP) and 20 per cent of government budgets in education during the past 40 years.[4] While the investment throughout the MENA region has been substantial, the development in the GCC has been extraordinary.

Until the mid-1970s, higher education in the Gulf was largely limited to national institutions established following the discovery of oil. The first significant expansion occurred in Saudi Arabia, with seven major universities built by 2005. Recent reports suggest that planned institutions may soon bring the number to 28, with projections for 10 additional universities by 2020.[5] Growth has not been limited to Saudi Arabia and, since the 1990s, projects such as University City in Sharjah, Academic City in Dubai, and Education City in Doha have contributed to the increasing number of newly established institutions and branch campuses throughout the GCC.

This article provides an overview of the architectural approaches employed in the first institutions in the GCC, including King Saud University and the University of Qatar. It also covers Masdar Institute and the King Abdullah University of Science and Technology – two recently developed postgraduate institutions focused on sustainability-related research.

Early Campus Design

As mentioned above, the first major universities in the Gulf were in Saudi Arabia. King Saud University was initially founded as the University of Riyadh in 1957. In the 1970s Karl Schwanzer, an Austrian architect perhaps best known for the BMW Administration Building in Munich (1972), developed a comprehensive masterplan for the King Saud University campus.[6] Following Schwanzer's death in 1975, Hellmuth, Obata & Kassabaum (HOK) was commissioned to lead a consortium to further develop the masterplan and design the campus buildings. Although revisions to the original programme led to adaptations, Schwanzer's original masterplan remained largely intact.

The campus comprises a central core containing a large open atrium, administrative offices, library and auditoria, and radiating spines that serve as pedestrian connections to the academic buildings that are linked to the spines via an internal 'street' running through each building. In terms of architectural expression, the architects relied on a precast concrete system that was adapted to incorporate visual references to traditional buildings in the Najd region.

The founding of King Saud University was followed by the King Fahd University for Petroleum and Minerals and King Abdulaziz University in the 1960s. King Fahd University was designed by US-based Caudill Rowlett Scott, the firm that also provided structural and civil engineering services as a member of the HOK-led consortium commissioned to design King Saud University. Located on a hilltop site overlooking Dhahran, the original campus plan consists of a series of buildings arranged to respond to the topography and to create internal courts.

The original University of Qatar campus (1983), designed by Kamal El Kafrawi, is a significant example of an early attempt to develop a contextual approach to campus planning.[7] Except for buildings housing the administration, student activities and ancillary services, the initial phase of the campus was developed according to a series of octagonal modules arranged according to an 8.40-by-8.40-metre (27.56-by-27.56-foot) grid interspersed with 3.48-by-3.48-metre (11.42-by-11.42-foot) modules. Academic buildings do not exceed two floors, while the library is three storeys in height to indicate its primary role as the symbolic 'centre' of the campus. The octagonal modules used for the library and the academic buildings are capped with a square wind-tower-like element that mediates light and facilitates airflow in the open spaces; when the modules are combined to create larger open spaces, precast roof trusses or cast-in-place folded plates are used. In addition to region-specific visual references such as the wind tower, grilles throughout the project recall *mashrabiya* (interlaced screens used to control light, reduce glare, facilitate airflow and maintain privacy).

Hok+4 Consortium (Hellmuth, Obata & Kassabaum, Gollins Melvin Ward Partnership, Syska & Hennessy, Dames & Moore And Claudill Rowlett Scott), King Saud University, Riyadh, Saudi Arabia, 1984

The exterior circulation spines connecting academic buildings at King Saud University are covered by a precast concrete system that forms a colonnade defined by a series of planar arches.

Kamal El Kafrawi with Arup Associates, University of Qatar, Doha, Qatar, 1983

The University of Qatar comprises a system based on octagonal modules capped by wind-tower-like elements that facilitate airflow and allow for natural light.

Foster + Partners,
Masdar Institute,
Abu Dhabi, UAE,
2010

Three- to four-storey buildings provide shade throughout the day and define the narrow street-like spaces that join the open plazas.

Contemporary Approaches to Persistent Challenges

While earlier campus projects relied primarily on passive measures to mediate the climate, the significant technological advances in the past 20 years and the increasing emphasis on sustainability have impacted the design of educational institutions in the Gulf. The Masdar Institute in Abu Dhabi and the King Abdullah University of Science and Technology (KAUST), located just outside Jeddah in Thuwal, are prime examples of attempts to integrate both active systems and passive strategies to reduce the impact of the climate on resource consumption.

The Masdar Institute, designed by Foster + Partners, was planned as an integral component of Masdar City, a 7-square-kilometre (3-square-mile) low-rise, high-density urban area intended to be one of the most sustainable cities in the world. Although the 2008 financial crisis slowed development of Masdar City, the Masdar Institute was completed in 2010. Developed in collaboration with the Massachusetts Institute of Technology (MIT), the institution is described as the world's first graduate-level university focused on solutions to sustainability-related challenges. The institution's mandate and mission are reflected in the sustainable solutions integrated into the campus plan and the individual buildings.

Academic buildings sit on a 7-metre (23-foot) podium that accommodates high-performance laboratories, clean rooms and essential infrastructure, including the service system for personal rapid transit (PRT) vehicles intended to replace cars. Buildings are arranged to create a series of narrow alleys and open plazas, one of which contains a large-scale wind tower with integrated mist generators to direct breezes down into the open court. In addition to a range of active systems, Masdar Institute buildings employ a number of passive measures, such as louvres and glass-reinforced concrete (GRC) screens to block direct solar radiation and allow airflow. Buildings rely on natural ventilation during cooler months – air enters into the ground floor and, as it is heated, rises and escapes through openings on the upper floor.

Foster + Partners,
Masdar Institute,
Abu Dhabi, UAE,
2010

above: Climate-responsive measures at Masdar Institute include curtain-wall facades on laboratory buildings that employ ethylene tetrafluoroethylene (ETFE) cushions and glass-reinforced concrete (GRC) panels that form *mashrabiya*-like screens for shading.

below: The level 01 floor plan shows the interior configuration of interior spaces, the distribution of academic buildings, and the relation between narrow street-like spaces and open plazas.

At just over 500,000 square metres (5,382,000 square feet), which is more than 10 times larger than the Masdar Institute, KAUST is a postgraduate institution concerned with sustainability-related research, with a specific focus on water, food, energy and the environment. Designed by HOK, the campus is organised around a central axis that extends from the main entry through the administrative building and a multi-tiered plaza containing the library and campus mosque. The plaza, which opens out onto Safaa Harbour and provides views of the Red Sea beyond, is bounded on the northwest and southeast sides by clusters that contain research labs, a student centre and the data centre. Research labs, arranged in a four-square configuration, are linked by covered street-like spaces.

KAUST earned a LEED Platinum rating for an array of sustainability-related measures that are impressive in scope and scale: 75 per cent of all construction waste was recycled; 100 per cent of wastewater is reused; annual energy cost has been lowered by approximately 27 per cent; and overall water use has been reduced by 42 per cent.[8] A series of active and passive strategies was employed to mediate the impact of the climate. Vertical 'solar towers' sheathed in a double-glazed skin supported by a precast concrete diagrid structure punctuate the research building clusters. Superheating the towers to accelerate airflow, combined with cooling from misting devices, assists in maintaining comfort in the exterior spaces between research buildings.

MECCA   NORTH

Masdar University - Level 01 Plan

0   5   10m

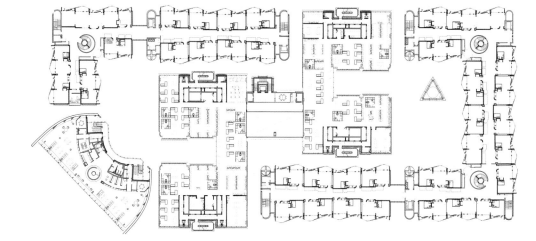

HOK,
King Abdullah University of Science
and Technology (KAUST),
Thuwal, Saudi Arabia,
2009

top: The centre of the KAUST campus
is a multi-tiered plaza that
provides views of the Red Sea.

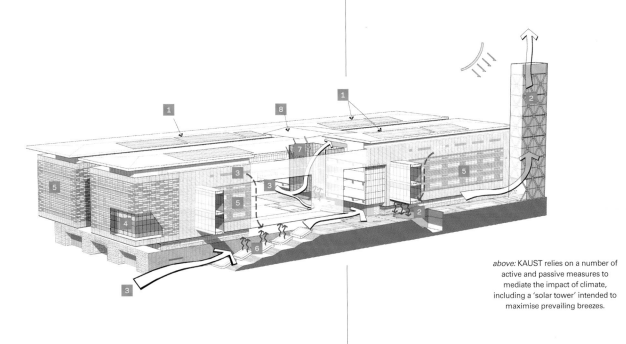

above: KAUST relies on a number of
active and passive measures to
mediate the impact of climate,
including a 'solar tower' intended to
maximise prevailing breezes.

HOK,
King Abdullah University
of Science and Technology
(KAUST),
Thuwal, Saudi Arabia,
2009

Academic buildings at KAUST are
covered by a massive roof structure
designed to accommodate solar
arrays and punctuated by interior-
focused atria.

Campus Cities

As Ameena Ahmadi discusses in her article on Education City in Doha in this issue of *D* (pp 46–53), the expansion of educational opportunities in the GCC has given rise to branch campuses within enclaves planned to host educational institutions from abroad. Although similar enterprises such as Academic City and Knowledge Village in Dubai have been developed, the level of quality of design and construction that is evident in the Qatar Foundation's flagship project has not been matched elsewhere.

In contrast to Education City's collection of individual buildings that are differentiated by a variety of architectural expressions, Sharjah's University City comprises indigenous institutions rather than branch campuses and is characterised by the stylistic cohesiveness resulting from the centralised approval processes that govern the appearance of buildings. Containing two comprehensive universities, a teaching hospital and other educational institutions, University City is organised along an axis defined by a 4-kilometre (2.5-mile) boulevard that concludes at the American University of Sharjah campus. While projects such as Masdar Institute and KAUST rely on tight-knit circulation networks and internal courts found in vernacular precedents, the open plazas and insistent adherence to strict formal ordering systems result in outwardly focused buildings that privilege their representative function.

Future Projects and Prospects

A number of new educational projects are planned or are presently under construction, including new buildings for Kuwait University's Sabah Al Salem University City: the College of Arts and College of Education buildings by Perkins+Will/Dar Al-Handasah (Shair and Partners); the College for Women, College of Business Administration and College of Engineering (Cambridge Seven Associates); Main Administration Building (Skidmore, Owings & Merrill); and Faculty Housing (RAFT Architects). The recently completed Princess Nora Bint Abdulrahman University designed by Perkins+Will/Dar Al-Handasah (Shair and Partners) in Riyadh is described as the largest university for women in the world and is projected to serve 60,000 female undergraduate students.[9] Projects such as this provide an indication of the perceived demand that results from the GCC's youth bulge and demonstrate the commitment to educating the region's population.

Architectural quality varies significantly across institutions in the GCC, and a review of contemporary projects indicates that many struggle with the question of responsiveness to context and appropriateness of expression. Some architects have responded to context-related concerns by referencing 'traditional' building elements and/or drawing inspiration from historical settlement patterns; however, the increasing scale and complexity of educational institutions poses challenges. While the distant past offers many lessons, there is also much to learn from more recent examples that are sensitive to scale, context and climate, such as Kamal El Kafrawi's design for the University of Qatar campus.

Despite the qualitative differences in the design and construction of educational projects, the commitment to higher education and the increasing awareness of sustainability in the GCC's resource-scarce environment form a strong foundation for future development. In *Place and Experience*, Jeff Maplas writes: 'Indeed, the social does not exist prior to place nor is it given expression except in and through place … It is within the structure of place that the very possibility of the social arises.'[10] Maplas points out the reciprocal relationship between structure of place and the structure of social relations – in this respect, the design of educational institutions can contribute to the advancement of knowledge and, in turn, to transformations at both individual and collective levels. The significant investment in higher education institutions in the GCC has already enhanced the lives of many individual students, and it has the potential to foster broader change in the future if there is also investment in developing knowledge-based economies that recognise talent and reward initiative. Ð

Notes
1. The following sources provide general introductions to education in the region: George Makdisi, *The Rise of Colleges: Institutions of Learning in Islam and the West*, Edinburgh University Press (Edinburgh), 1981; Osama Abi-Mershed, *Trajectories of Education in the Arab World: Legacies and Challenges*, Routledge (London), 2010.
2. Barry Mirkin, 'Arab Spring: Demographics in a Region in Transition', *Arab Human Development Report Research Paper Series*, United Nations Development Programme (New York), 2013, p 13: www.arab-hdr.org/publications/other/ahdrps/AHDR%20ENG%20Arab%20Spring%20Mirkinv3.pdf.
3. The Economist Intelligence Unit, *The GCC in 2020, The Gulf and its People*, The Economist Intelligence Unit (London, New York and Hong Kong), 2009, p 9: http://graphics.eiu.com/upload/eb/Gulf2020part2.pdf.
4. World Bank, *The Road Not Traveled: Education Reform in the Middle East and Africa*, World Bank (Washington DC), 2008, p 3: http://siteresources.worldbank.org/INTMENA/Resources/EDU_Flagship_Full_ENG.pdf.
5. Beatrice Thomas, 'Saudi to Get 3 More Universities, ArabianBusiness.com, 3 April 2014: www.arabianbusiness.com/saudi-get-3-more-universities-545021.html.
6. A comprehensive description of the project is provided by the architects in 'Saudi Arabia: King Saud University', in Hasan-Uddin Khan (ed), *Mimar 42: Architecture in Development*, Concept Media Ltd (London), 1992, pp 48–50.
7. For an assessment of the University of Qatar campus, see Romi Kholsa, *Technical Review Summary, University of Qatar (380.QAT)*, Aga Khan Award for Architecture (Geneva), 1992.
8. www.hok.com/design/type/science-technology/king-abdullah-university-of-science-and-technology/.
9. www.pnuproject.com.
10. JE Malpas, *Place and Experience: A Philosophical Topography*, Cambridge University Press (Cambridge), 1999, p 36.

Francis Gambert,
American University of Sharjah,
Sharjah, UAE,
1997

The American University of Sharjah concludes a 4-kilometre (2.5-mile) long axis that defines University City. The campus comprises outwardly focused buildings that privilege their representational function.

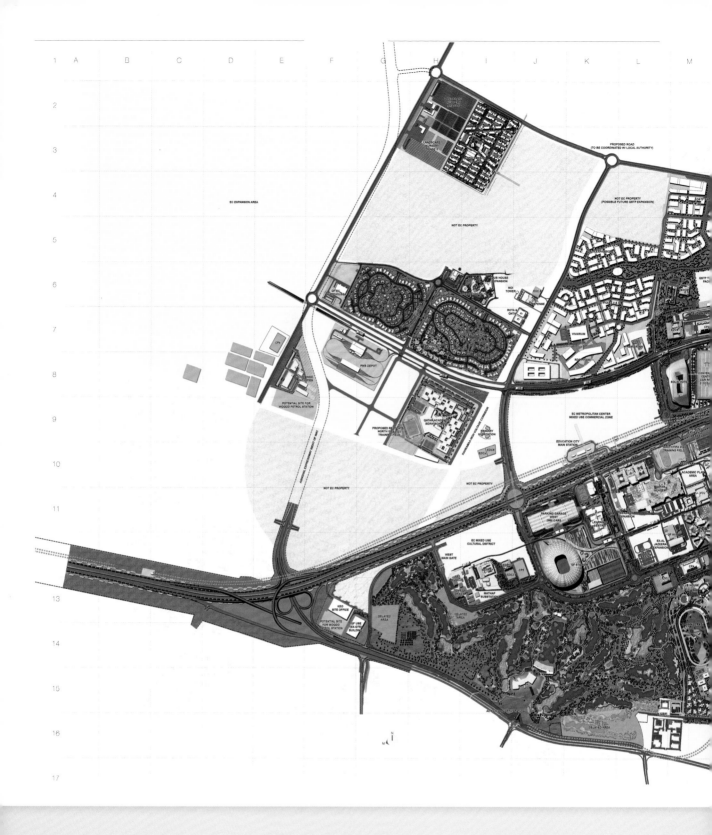

Qatar Foundation,
Education City Masterplan,
Doha, Qatar,
2014

Education City Masterplan v. 18
demonstrating the entire development
including completed and future projects
as well as landscaping.

Ameena Ahmadi

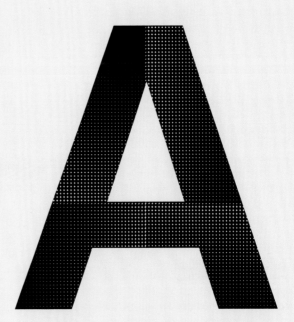

A
City for Education

Ameena Ahmadi is Architecture Manager at the Qatar Foundation, overseeing the development of the masterplan and facilities of Education City in Doha, a multi-institution educational campus, incorporating schools and universities. Ahmadi describes how education is a significant cornerstone for Qatar's national transition 'to a knowledge-based' economy from a 'hydrocarbon-based' one. This is symbolised by substantial investment in the flagship Education City with its Arata Isozaki masterplan and its individual schools and universities designed by premier international architects.

Alongside appreciation of the prosperity the State of Qatar is currently experiencing, thanks to its oil and gas wealth, comes the acknowledgement that these resources will not last forever. The need to diversify the state's economy and shift from a hydrocarbon-based economy to a knowledge-based one is a key stipulation of the Qatar National Vision (QNV) 2030 and the Qatar National Development Strategy (QNDS) 2011–2016.[1] Future sustainability will be highly dependent on building competency and competing globally. Human development is hence identified as one of four pillars for the QNV 2030, with an emphasis on building a healthy and educated population. Educational reform is therefore key in achieving this vision, and the growth of Education City, the Qatar Foundation's flagship development, is an important step in this process.

The Qatar Foundation, established in 1995 by His Highness Sheikh Hamad bin Khalifa Al Thani and chaired by his wife, Sheikha Moza bint Nasser, was developed to support projects in the areas of education, science and community development.[2] Part of the mandate of the Qatar Foundation is realised through Education City, a multi-institution campus established in what was a sparsely populated residential area in the northwestern outskirts of Doha. Education City currently contains seven branch campuses and several other homegrown institutes and faculties. With a growing young population in Qatar, its programmes offer an alternative for Qataris as well as students from the wider region and abroad.[3] Serving a current student population of over 5,000[4] and planned to cater for 11,000, Education City is assisting the state's development in education and research while also investing heavily in health and innovation infrastructures.

Education City began with Qatar Academy, a single school offering primary, middle and international baccalaureate diploma programmes along with an early-childhood centre, in 1995. The construction of the academy was followed by buildings for the Qatar Foundation Headquarters and a facility for Virginia Commonwealth University (VCU), all of which were designed by local architectural consultancies to resemble the traditional architecture of Qatar and the region. Although initial plans for the area now known as Education City focused on small-scale development around Qatar Academy, an expansion of the mandate of the Foundation led to the commissioning of Arata Isozaki to develop the first masterplan covering a wider precinct and functions.

Developed in 2001, Isozaki's plan was devised around a Green Spine, which became a key organising element and a north–south connector across various functions. Academic buildings and the Qatar Foundation's new headquarters were located to the east and west of the Green Spine, which

Illustration of the rapid growth of Education City from 300 hectares (750 acres) in 2001 to over 1,500 hectares (3,700 acres) in 2014.

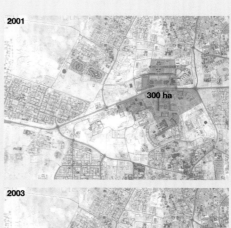

2001

300 ha

2003

614 ha

2004

754 ha

2014

1,500 ha

ends at the south with an outdoor celebration court, and at the north with the Qatar National Convention Centre. Education City is divided into a northern zone and a southern zone by a main vehicular road, Luqta Street. Public-oriented venues, a large teaching and specialised hospital along with research facilities are concentrated in the north, while academic functions are clustered in the southern zone. Several revisions have since been made to the masterplan to accommodate Education City's continuous expansion, from an area of approximately 300 hectares (750 acres) when Isozaki first planned it to approximately 1,500 hectares (3,700 acres) as it stands today.

The appointment of Isozaki to develop the masterplan for Education City resulted from the Qatar Foundation's commitment to ensuring design quality. This was further demonstrated through selecting internationally renowned architects to design the various buildings for the Education City campus, including Ricardo and Victor Legorreta, Sir David Chipperfield, Rem Koolhaas/OMA, Antoine Predock, Jason Moriyama, Cesar Pelli and Fred Clarke. The brief provided by the Foundation focuses on two points: that environments for learning and innovation should be pleasant atmospheres designed to the highest standards, and that a building in Education City is not a common building, but an opportunity to exhibit and learn about architecture itself. To illustrate its vision for architecture of education, four diverse types are discussed below through projects that are either completed or under construction, each representing a commitment to ensuring that the architecture in Education City both supports education and provides opportunities for learning about the potential of good design.

The Insular

After creating the initial masterplan for Education City, Isozaki was also commissioned to design four facilities on campus, among them the Liberal Arts and Science (LAS) Building. Isozaki's projects were the first contemporary efforts at reinterpreting traditional architecture following the early buildings that had adopted the vernacular through literal expressions. The LAS Building was completed in 2004, and designed in partnership with i-Net and Kazuhiro Kojima + Kazuko Akamatsu/C+A, to house the Academic Bridge Program, which offers general arts and science courses to assist high-school graduates' transition to university education. Climatic conditions such as Qatar's harsh temperatures were a key factor in designing the project. The architects conceived of the building as an insular block protected by a double-skin facade with small perforations that offer limited views to the exterior yet allow the building itself to illuminate at night. Six main courtyards are carved out of the building mass, providing views and daylight to classrooms and other

Arata Isozaki,
i-Net and Kazuhiro
Kojima + Kazuko Akamatsu/C+A,
Liberal Arts and Science
(LAS) Building, Education City,
Doha, Qatar,
2004

top: Interior of the LAS Building showing the multiple levels of transparency. The ground level, which contains learning spaces, offers greater degrees of transparency, whereas the upper floor is surrounded by a mesh of screens creating a quiet zone for offices.

bottom: Northern facade of the LAS Building showing the quasi-crystalline pattern that wraps the building mass. The six towers that rise from the building's courtyards and ventilate the car park at the basement level are inspired by the wind towers that appear in traditional architecture throughout the Gulf, making a visual connection to Qatar's past.

spaces. Incorporating different layers of transparency is another main feature, expressed at different degrees on each level of the building. The 'insular' is also wrapped by a continuous pattern, made by a quasi-crystal structure, which is based on geometrical arrangements found in the architecture and art of the Muslim world.

The Connected

After designing two buildings for two different branch campuses, Legorreta + Legorreta were commissioned to design another two facilities: an academic building and a student centre for the entire campus. It was not a straightforward task to design a students' facility for a diverse population in a university of universities, within a campus under construction, given the dynamic conditions of the surroundings and multiple requirements of the users. The scheme for the Hamad bin Khalifa University (HBKU)[5] Student Center therefore needed to consider the partially developed context and anticipate connections to what will come in the future. Permeability and variation were two key principles on which Legorreta + Legorreta based the scheme, and this was achieved by making the building an intersection that permeates movement across different destinations.

Vernacular town plans in Qatar and the Arab region inspired the spatial configuration of the project, where alleys link its different components, enhancing its overall connectivity. The alleys are enclosed by a repetitive umbrella-column structure that surrounds a central sculpture garden and connects the building's various functions. The building was designed to facilitate movement and allow users to engage in independent and group activities in settings that range from public to private. Completed in 2011 with a total area of 34,000 square metres (365,970 square feet), the facility offers spaces for general services, a food court, and sports and leisure.

The Public

In a growing campus like Education City, creating a central library that offers shared resources for students of all faculties along with researchers and faculty members was essential. The project was initially planned as a central campus library; however, it was soon designated the Qatar National Library (2015). When appointed for the project, Rem Koolhaas and OMA continued questioning and reconsidering the function of a traditional library following their own precedent in the Seattle Central Library in the US (2004).

OMA started the project, which has an area of approximately 46,000 square metres (495,000 square feet), by questioning issues like information accessibility, ease of physical browsing and ease of cataloguing and sorting. Formal explorations then led to a scheme tiled 'Book Arena' that offered a great deal of visibility within the library interiors, a factor that could make it an ideal public facility. The form is the result of

Legorreta + Legorreta,
Hamad bin Khalifa University (HBKU)
Student Center, Education City,
Doha, Qatar,
2011

top: The Sculpture Garden is wrapped in a screen designed in collaboration with artist Jan Hendrix: an example of integrating art with architecture in Education City.

bottom: The column structure at the southwestern entryway is repeated throughout the building, both indoors and outdoors.

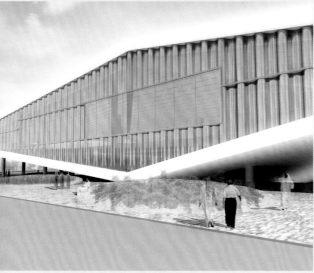

OMA,
Qatar National Library,
Education City,
Doha, Qatar,
2014

top: The open-plan library showing the book tiers and the bridge that connects them with the various study areas.

left: Southern facade of the library that will act as an urban hub with a stop for the campus tram system.

Mangera Yvars Architects (MYAA),
Qatar Faculty of
Islamic Studies (QFIS)
and Education City Mosque,
Education City,
Doha, Qatar,
2014

top:
The dynamic form of the building and its
different-sized courtyards.

bottom:
The QFIS southeastern facade, where two
minarets rising at heights of 60 metres (200
feet) and 75 metres (250 feet) mark an eastern
gateway to Education City.

three main folds of a basic square plane: two folds on two corners, and a longer fold on an edge, resulting in a central triangular-shaped space that serves as the library's public plaza. Although an introverted building with select direct connections to the outside, the library creates an interior urban space for the Education City community and the community at large. The folded corners and edge create a tiered interior shelving area for the library's collection and also act as the main entry points to the library. A bridge spans the full length of the library, connecting the book tiers and accommodating the study spaces.

The Avant-Garde

Though differing significantly in appearance from the mosques currently found in Qatar, the Qatar Faculty of Islamic Studies and Education City Mosque (2014) takes much of its inspiration from the traditional architecture of the Arab and Muslim world. Here, Ada Yvars Bravo and Ali Mangera of Mangera Yvars Architects (MYAA) aimed to reinterpret elements of the great edifices of the Muslim world in a contemporary language. The

approach was in line with the Qatar Foundation's vision for the project, that requested the revival of the traditional madrasa model, in which seeking knowledge and worship are combined in one complex. MYAA began their concept studies with the metaphor of knowledge leading to enlightenment reflected in two ribbons: a ribbon of knowledge and a ribbon of light. The two intertwine, creating a dynamic form with a lower sweeping mass of classrooms and a higher volume for the mosque, ending with the 'ribbons' then ascending towards the sky marking the minarets of Education City mosque. Courtyards within the classroom and office volumes ensure that every space in the faculty has access to daylight and a view to a landscaped area. Four 'rivers' run through the interior and exterior spaces of the building, echoing the rivers mentioned in the Quran.

Building Foundations

Building Education City has required a complex process of collaboration that involves numerous architects, consultants and stakeholders. Projects are designed in collaboration with the users to ensure that their specific programme requirements are met while maintaining the level of quality that the Qatar Foundation envisions. Through ongoing dialogue and debate, the Foundation, the architects and users continuously inform the process from inception to completion. Though with each new project another exemplary piece of architecture is created for education and research, building Education City has been a tremendous task given the fast pace of the development, the diversity of contributors as well as the constant expansion of the Qatar Foundation's programmes.

Due to the incremental growth of the campus, the first few academic buildings, such as LAS, were realised as self-contained blocks. Self-sufficient buildings offering the required services within were important in the absence of shared functions at the start of the project. More recent planned and completed projects offer higher degrees of permeability and interdependence with other shared facilities across Education City. In all cases, spaces for learning benefit from a visible investment in informal spaces of exchange. Each branch campus and faculty is equipped with classrooms and facilities similar to those found in other highly ranked institutes worldwide, but what becomes unique in Education City is the generosity in turning corridors and common areas into casual spots for learning and exchange. Niches are allocated in some cases as informal spillover learning areas, with corridors widened to include additional seating and artwork for informal meetings to continue beyond the classroom.

What has been achieved thus far in Education City has been recognised as a unique national, regional and global destination that is currently designated as one of four metropolitan centres for the greater city of Doha. Education City's masterplan remains a work in progress, however, with a current agenda of increasing connectivity, both internally and to the wider city. Pedestrian connections, for example, are being designed to provide a comfortable transition between Education City's landmark buildings. The urban life created within the buildings is yet to manifest in the landscape and outdoor spaces in between. Green parks, gardens and playgrounds that afford outdoor life within the campus are still being developed and will take time to mature. Although dependent on cars now, the campus is intended to be even more pedestrian friendly in the future with the elimination of vehicles within, and the use of public transport instead. To further improve this envisaged pedestrian life, landscaping schemes using a palette of local and near-local species are under development. Connecting Education City to various destinations across the city of Doha is also underway as part of the planned Qatar metro scheme, where four major stations will be located at the parameter of the campus. Overall, the journey of building Education City has certainly been one of building an organisation, building connections and knowledge exchange. ⌂

Notes
1. Both documents were published by the General Secretariat for Development Planning in 2008 (QNV 2030) and in 2011 (QNDS 2011-2016). They are available online at www.gsdp.gov.qa/portal/page/portal/gsdp_en.
2. More information is available on the Qatar Foundation website: www.qf.org.qa.
3. Education City branch campuses are open for students from all around the world to apply, based on similar requirements as the home campuses of these colleges. The programmes are an alternative to Qatar University and other smaller colleges in the state. They are also a convenient alternative to travelling abroad for Qataris and residents of Qatar.
4. As of June 2014.
5. Hamad bin Khalifa University (HBKU) is an emerging research university established by the Qatar Foundation that will deliver Master's and Doctoral programmes through interdisciplinary colleges. For more information visit www.hbku.edu.qa. The Student Center is led by HBKU and serves the whole of Education City, including all of the existing branch campuses.

The Evolution of Tall Building in the Gulf

Terri Meyer Boake

Skidmore, Owings &
Merrill (SOM)

Burj Khalifa

Dubai, UAE

2010

At 828 metres (2,716 feet),
this building remains the
tallest in the world,
surpassing the record
of 508 metres (1,667 feet)
set by Taipei 101 in 2004.
As a point of comparison,
the Makkah Royal Clock
Tower Hotel in Saudi
Arabia achieved 601 metres
(1,972 feet) in 2012.

From the Sensational to the Sensitive

In just 35 years the built environment in the Gulf region has evolved so rapidly that it has gone from having no high-rise buildings to having the world's tallest building – SOM's Burj Khalifa in Dubai. **Terri Meyer Boake**, a professor at the University of Waterloo in Ontario and specialist in steel construction and skyscraper design, provides an overview of the fast-paced development of this building typology.

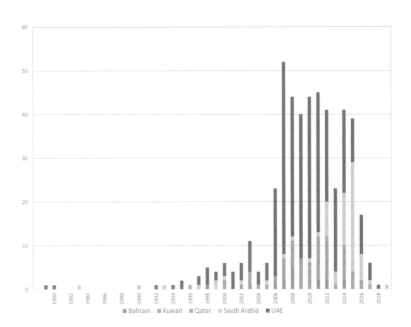

Tall Buildings in the Gulf Region by Country, 1979-2019

The UAE's production of tall buildings leads the other Gulf-region countries into the 21st century although activity is increasing in Saudi Arabia.

, Harris and Partners,
, Rashid Tower,
, Trade Centre,
, UAE,

, skyscraper in the Gulf
, ed 149 metres (489 feet) in
, nd comprised 39 floors.
, d to mitigate the severe
, the deep precast concrete
, provided protection from
, d solar radiation.

It is almost inconceivable that Dubai first had electricity in 1952 and, by 2010 with the completion of the Burj Khalifa at 828 metres (2,716 feet) high, the city claimed the world's tallest building – an accomplishment unsurpassed to this date. When this landmark achievement is eclipsed by the Kingdom Tower in Jeddah – expected to reach 1,000 metres (3,280 feet) in 2019 – the record will continue to reside in the Middle East. In a world whose architectural achievements in the past centuries have been dominated by the West, the shift eastward is significant.

Designed as part of Dubai's World Trade Centre complex and completed in 1979, the Sheikh Rashid Tower was the first skyscraper to be constructed in the Gulf region. It was designed by John R Harris, a British architect whose contributions to the development of Dubai are discussed by Todd Reisz on pp 100–5 of this issue). Situated in isolation and surrounded by desert, the building served as a destination for viewing the emerging city. However, it has long since been dwarfed by other towers constructed during the building boom. In terms of overall height, as of August 2014 the Skyscraper Center Database maintained by the Council on Tall Buildings and Urban Habitat (CTBUH) ranked the Sheikh Rashid Tower 164th of the 269 listed skyscrapers in Dubai, and 246th compared to all skyscrapers in the Middle East region.[1]

It is difficult to avoid a focus on statistics when discussing tall buildings. Size matters, and so do quantities. The architecture of tall buildings was for a long time a solely North American enterprise, but this ceased to be the case when development in China and the Middle East began to escalate in the 1980s. By 2000, North America accounted for less than half of the 100 tallest buildings in the world.[2] Structural materiality changed from a domination of steel, which was plentiful in the northeastern US, to concrete and composite construction as towers became taller and the nature of the workforce adapted to the global availability of materials and the local knowledge in the construction industry. Databases shifted from counting all tall buildings, to those with a minimum height of 150 metres (490 feet), and then to 200 metres (660 feet) as the quantities increased to such an extent as to verge on becoming difficult to track. Buildings that would have once qualified as being tall no longer do.

Skidmore, Owings & Merrill (SOM)

National Commercial Bank

Jeddah, Saudi Arabia

1983

This inward-looking tower acknowledges the harsh desert climate through its use of a solid mass facing the exterior, and glazed facades opening on to internally focused voids.

NORR Architects, Engineers and Planners

Emirates Towers One and Two

Dubai, UAE

1980

The paired towers were situated to form a gateway to the city. The Sheikh Rashid Tower is visible in the background.

Atkins

Burj Al Arab

Dubai, UAE

1999

The spectacular seven-star hotel demonstrated that Dubai could compete globally. The decoration, form and colours of the atrium fancifully incorporated visual references from the region.

The precast facade system used by Harris in the Sheikh Rashid Tower combined similar construction methods to that in use in Western architecture of the period, but with a more expressive appearance characterised by arched openings and an interplay of shadow and light resulting from the depth of the facade. The 27-storey National Commercial Bank in Jeddah designed by Skidmore, Owings & Merrill (SOM) and completed in 1983 created a unique vertical version of a traditional courtyard typology. The solid exterior walls were interrupted by three triangular voids cut into the building to form courtyards. The office windows were oriented into the voids, which allowed interior spaces to have natural light without heat gain and glare. Both Harris and SOM made overt use of solar avoidance to increase comfort in ways that were in keeping with methods that are traditional to the region. This was not the case with subsequent facade design, and by the time of the building boom in the 2000s, thin, sleek glass and metal curtain-wall systems had long replaced facades that incorporated passive shading.

Skidmore, Owings &
Merrill (SOM),
National Commercial Bank
Jeddah, Saudi Arabia,
1983

During the two decades following the completion of the Dubai World Trade Centre and the National Commercial Bank, tall building construction in the Gulf region was relatively limited. The completion of the Burj Al Arab by Atkins in 1999 marks the beginning of the age of skyscrapers in the Gulf Region. In 2000, NORR Architects' Emirates Towers One and Two formed the new gates to modern Dubai. But it was truly the spectacle of the Burj Al Arab, a high-end sail-shaped luxury hotel, which put Dubai on the architectural map. While other Gulf countries also focused on new buildings, the United Arab Emirates, and especially Dubai, emerged as the region's leader.

NORR Architects,
Engineers and Planners,
Emirates Towers One and
Dubai, UAE,
1980

The rapid pace of development in the Gulf resulted in an influx of architectural practices from abroad as markets elsewhere had slowed. The region was also attractive as commercial tall buildings in other places were usually constrained by tight budgets and often uninspired clients who were unwilling to take risks. With no history of building tall, there was a need to import expertise. Some Gulf countries also have graduated licensing for architects, making the acquisition of a special tall building licence a requirement, which has encouraged the use of non-Gulf-based firms with established tall building experience for this specialised work.

Facilitated by ever-larger budgets, the new era of the tall building in the Middle East became highly competitive as each project attempted to distinguish itself from the others in unique ways – by shape, cladding, geometric form or height. The timing of the initial surge in development, in retrospect, was problematic as the substantial budgets, combined with the desire for sleek structures, resulted in buildings that were undifferentiated from those found elsewhere. This led to the early adoption of extensive glazing using standard curtain-wall systems

cp. use of light + hills etc.

that were entirely reliant on air conditioning for cooling. In 2000, Western architecture was only on the cusp of aspiring to sustainable skyscrapers, so there were few high-performance buildings to mimic and virtually nothing that had been constructed in a severely hot-arid-humid climate. The climate in the Gulf is unusual as the desert is situated in a subtropical climate, resulting in extraordinarily high levels of humidity, in a region with little or no access to fresh water and dependency on desalination. As a result of the difference between the air temperature and the temperature of air-conditioned interior spaces, the dust in the air tends to stick to glazed exteriors that have reached their dew point. The lack of fresh water makes the cleaning of buildings difficult and expensive. This problem is exacerbated by geometrically complex facades that cannot make use of traditional cleaning stages.

With over 400 skyscrapers completed in the Gulf, the majority constructed between 1999 and 2014, what sets some apart or above others? Nominally they could be grouped into three categories: the 'stars', the fabric and the visionary (unbuilt). However, a more critical review of the development of high-rise buildings in the Gulf region reveals that there have been technically progressive contributions to the overall development of the skyscraper type.

Atkins,
Burj Al Arab,
Dubai, UAE,
1999

Technical Advancements

The substantial budgets and aspirations behind many projects in the Gulf have provided global benefits to the advancement of tall building design and construction. And the desires of the projects have been effective in pushing the boundaries of existing technologies into new realms.

Whereas more conservative projects have been unable to push height records beyond those of the Willis (Sears) Tower (442 metres/1,450 feet) in Chicago (1974) and the original World Trade Center Towers (417 metres/1,368 feet) in New York (1973), the success of the 828-metre (2,716-foot) Burj Khalifa in setting a new world record for height advanced wind engineering, concrete pumping and elevator technologies. The lessons learned in the Rowan Williams Davies & Irwin (RWDI) boundary layer wind tunnels during the design development of the Burj Khalifa have been used to inform decisions made on other projects. Over 40 wind-tunnel tests were conducted on the Burj Khalifa, including large structural analysis models and facade pressure tests, microclimate analysis at the terraces and around the tower base. Temporary conditions during the construction stage were tested with the tower cranes to ensure safety. The setback style of the Y-shaped plan provides a buttress-like stiffness to the tower, and the spiral design of the placement of the setbacks, based on the organic inspiration of the hymenocallis flower, reduces vortex shedding.

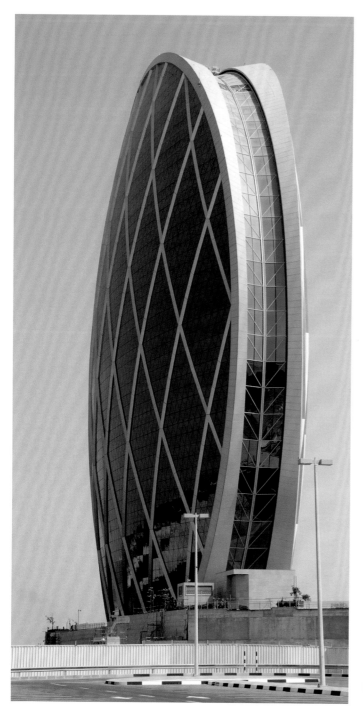

MZ Architects

Aldar Headquarters

Abu Dhabi, UAE

2010

The disc shape of this tower
is achieved through the use of
convex diagrid structures that
support the facade system.

Ateliers Jean Nouvel

Doha Tower

Doha, Qatar

2012

The entire tower is wrapped
in a shading layer that is
reminiscent of *mashrabiya*
screens to create a region-
specific approach to double
facade systems.

RMJM Architects

Capital Gate

Abu Dhabi, UAE

2011

This project took advantage of advancements in computer-assisted design to fabricate the 822 unique steel nodes that comprise the interior and exterior diagrid frames.

Constructability became a central issue in the Burj Khalifa as it was necessary to lift structural materials to never-before-contemplated heights. Even the 200-metre (660-foot) steel architectural spire required specialised prefabrication from within the top floors and was ultimately jacked into place. Concrete had never before been pumped to such a height.[3] Putzmeister was responsible for creating a system of specially designed pumps and runs that made exclusive use of high-compressive-strength concrete mixtures. Acknowledging the negative impact of hot daytime temperatures, all pours were done at night. The concrete was chilled in the plant prior to preparation, and part of the water was replaced with shards of ice, allowing the concrete to be transferred at 28°C (82°F).

Even the advanced elevator systems incorporated into the Burj Khalifa will not be sufficient to service the Kingdom Tower.[4] From the perspective of the occupant, the computer-controlled two-storey cabs used in Burj Khalifa have increased efficiency. The details yet to be solved pertain to the strength and weight of the cabling systems, combined with testing for failure within the vertical runs of a kilometre-high tower. Otis had designed a system for the Burj Khalifa that replaced steel ropes with polyurethane-coated belts and bulky motors with smaller gearless drives, eliminating the need for a large engine room. Otis is building a new test facility in preparation for the bid on Kingdom Tower. KONE installed the elevators on the 601-metre (1,972-foot) Makkah Royal Clock Tower Hotel in Saudi Arabia by Dar al-Handasah (Shair and Partners) (2012). They have constructed a 305-metre (1,000-foot) test facility drilled down into the ground. The technological advancements of this competition will benefit the vertical transportation systems for future generations of tall buildings.

The structural systems for tall buildings have evolved greatly over the past 20 years, and much of this development is visible in projects throughout the Gulf. Reinforced concrete is the most typical structural system used in the region, so deviations from this are significant. Of particular note are the towers that have explored the new steel diagrid system. The Tornado Tower by CICO Consulting Architects & Engineers /SIAT Architekten + Ingenieure München GmbH (Doha, 2008), Aldar Headquarters by MZ Architects (Abu Dhabi, 2010) and Doha Tower by Ateliers Jean Nouvel (Doha, 2012) use a diagrid structural system. The Doha Tower is of particular interest in its use of a concrete-filled steel tube system. The China State Construction Engineering Corporation served as the main contractor, which explains the transfer of this technology, very common in China, to the Gulf.

MZ Architects,
Aldar Headquarters,
Abu Dhabi, UAE,
2010

Ateliers Jean Nouvel,
Doha Tower,
Doha, Qatar,
2012

RMJM
Architects,
Capital Gate,
Abu Dhabi, UAE,
2011

RMJM Architects' Capital Gate in Abu Dhabi (2011) uses a hollow structural steel diagrid paired with a pre-tensioned, pre-cambered concrete core to create the furthest-backward-leaning tower in the world.[5] The 18-degree lean creates an offset of the office function at the base of the tower from the hotel function that additionally hangs off of a central atrium adjacent to the core, the elevator positioned in the only continuous vertical space in the tower.

The Environmentally Progressive
As discussed in Jeffrey Willis's article on sustainability in the Gulf (pp 114–19 of this issue), there has been an increasing recognition of the need for sustainability measures to be implemented. In terms of tall buildings, several extremely well-considered projects completed in recent years have addressed associated energy issues and advanced efforts to develop technologies that respond to the region's severely hot-humid climate.

Unlike some of the more artistically motivated sculptural visionary projects, many of which have been subsequently abandoned, the Bahrain World Trade Center by Atkins (2008) sets itself apart in its use of climate-based reasons to determine the sculpting of its forms. The integration of the commercial-sized wind turbines determined the shape of the pair of sail-like towers to funnel the wind through their central void, with the general orientation set to take advantage of the onshore breezes. Although performance data is not available for its characteristic wind turbines, the intention of the client was to showcase a commitment to reducing the use of fossil fuels.

Much of the effort in combating the severity of the climate lies in facade design. The successful ventures in the Gulf have focused on solar avoidance, either through double facade techniques that employ modernised versions of traditional *mashrabiya*-like screens, or through the incorporation of shading systems.

Although the upper hotel portion of Capital Gate uses a more typical dual glass double facade, the lower office portion employs a large shading screen that extends from below the cantilevered pool on the 19th floor to the base of the building, where it curves out in a sweep to provide a shading canopy over the passenger drop-off area. The mesh is 90 per cent open and blocks out 30 per cent of the solar radiation. The space between the facades must be cleaned by abseiling, whereby cleaners are suspended from ropes to access spaces that are difficult to reach.

The innovative award-winning technology used on the Al Bahr Towers in Abu Dhabi (2012), designed by Aedas, centres on a dynamic facade comprising over 1,000 individual shading devices, controlled by a building management system, that open and close according to the path of the sun. Each unit is made up of stretched PTFE panels driven

Aedas and Arup,
Abu Dhabi Investment
Council Headquarters,
Al Bahr Towers,
Abu Dhabi, UAE,
2012

Aedas and Arup

Abu Dhabi Investment
Council Headquarters

Al Bahr Towers

Abu Dhabi, UAE

2012

This project uses a mechanised
shading layer on the east, west
and south faces of its towers.

Reiser + Umemoto,
RUR Architecture

0-14 Tower

Dubai, UAE

2011

The shading system takes a
static approach to providing
solar avoidance through the
use of a perforated concrete
exoskeleton.

Foster + Partners

The Index

Dubai, UAE

2011

This mixed-use project sits
between the Burj Khalifa and the
Emirates Towers. With narrow
sides oriented east–west, the
building employs passive
strategies to mediate the effects
of climate.

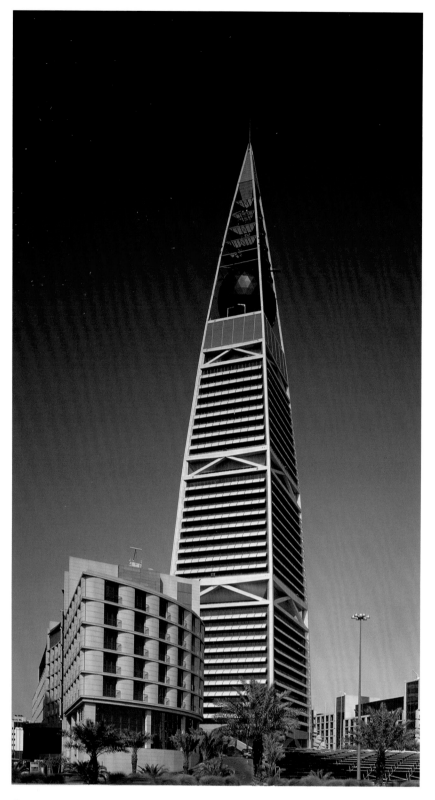

Foster + Partners

Al Faisaliyah Center

Riyadh, Saudi Arabia

2000

This was the first project to be completed by the firm in the region. It is oriented at approximately 45 degrees due north to create aesthetically more uniform shading requirements on the facades.

Skidmore, Owings & Merrill (SOM)

Al Hamra Firdous Tower

Kuwait City, Kuwait

2011

This is the tallest tower in Kuwait City. The complex geometries and varied facade treatments were developed in response to climate factors.

Goettsch Partners

Al Khatem Tower

Sowwah Square

Al Maryah Island

Abu Dhabi, UAE

2013

This project takes a comprehensive
approach to sustainable design
that includes landscape design,
massing, a double facade system
and strategic shading systems.

by a linear actuator. This provides a clearer view from the tower when solar gain is not an issue, and shading when the sun is to be avoided. The system is projected to reduce solar gain by 50 per cent and CO_2 emissions by 1,750 tonnes per year.[6]

The exterior skin of Jean Nouvel's Doha Tower is composed of four 'butterfly' aluminium elements of different scales to evoke the geometric complexity of the *mashrabiya* while serving as protection from the sun. The pattern varies according to the orientation and respective needs for solar protection: 25 per cent towards the north (the round plan of the tower requires shading on the north facade), 40 per cent towards the south, 60 per cent on the east and west. The variation in opacity of the aluminium screen addresses the variation in solar avoidance required on the facade orientations. The metal grating at the floor levels in the cavity provides additional shading.

Reiser + Umemoto,
RUR Architecture,
O-14 Tower,
Dubai, UAE,
2011

The innovative double facade system on Reiser + Umemoto's O-14 Tower (Dubai, 2010) places the insulated glazing layer on the interior, with the exterior layer provided by the concrete load-bearing shell. The perforated concrete exoskeleton is innovative in its use of digital and prefabrication technologies. The varied openings in the exterior skin provide for relatively unobstructed views from the floor-to-ceiling glazing. This achieves an unusual sense of openness while also protecting from the intensity of direct sunlight. This layering approach is similar to that used in the Doha Tower, and is beginning to emerge as a Gulf vernacular that shows a more comprehensive and sensitive approach to solar avoidance.

Foster + Partners,
The Index,
Dubai, UAE,
2011

Foster + Partners' The Index (Dubai, 2012) relies on a combination of orientation and deep shading devices to provide solar control. The narrow plan results in broad facades on the north and south, where solar control is easier to provide. To achieve its environmental strategies, the building was consciously oriented against the existing grid of the city generated by Sheikh Zayed Road. The environmental strategies also address the relationship of the building to its site by leaving an open, well-shaded atrium at the base that combines with a large water feature to create a cool microclimate. This permits acclimatisation as occupants transition between the interior and exterior spaces that is denied in most highly glazed typical lobby configurations. The shading strategy references Foster's earlier work on the Al Faisaliyah Center in Riyadh (2000), which was the first tower in Saudi Arabia. The project used anodised, sectional aluminium panels that were cantilevered to create sun shades.

Foster + Partners,
Al Faisaliyah Center,
Riyadh, Saudi Arabia,
2000

The form of SOM's Al Hamra Firdous Tower (Kuwait City, 2011) is cut from a prism, and a void taken from the centre and from each floor plate rotating anti-clockwise around the core. The massive southern core

Skidmore, Owings &
Merrill (SOM),
Al Hamra Firdous Tower,
Kuwait City, Kuwait,
2011

statistics in this article have been taken from
yscraper Center Database maintained by the
il on Tall Buildings and Urban Habitat (CTBUH)
skyscrapercenter.com) and are accurate as of
t 2014.

UH, Tall Buildings in Numbers: www.ctbuh.
blications/Journal/InNumbers/tabid/1108/
age/en-US/Default.aspx.

j Khalifa: Conquering the World's Tallest
ng', Putzmeisteramerica.com, 2 February 2010:
putzmeisteramerica.com/news/job-stories/
Khalifa---Conquering-the-Worlds-Tallest-
ngB.

Catts, 'Double-deck Elevators Rise as Tallest
s Test Limits', Bloomberg.com, 2 January 2013:
bloomberg.com/news/2013-01-02/double-deck-
ors-rise-as-tallest-towers-test-limits.html.

Schofield, 'Capital Gate, Abu Dhabi', CTBUH
al, Issue II, 2012, pp 12–17.

ncil on Tall Buildings and Urban Habitat
H), 'Al Bahar Towers, Abu Dhabi', January 2013:
ctbuh.org/TallBuildings/FeaturedTallBuildings/
edTallBuildingArchive2012/
arTowersAbuDhabi/tabid/3845/language/en-
fault.aspx.

ncil on Tall Buildings and Urban
t (CTBUH), 'Al Hamra Firdous Center,
t City', August 2013: www.ctbuh.
llBuildings/FeaturedTallBuildings/
edTallBuildingArchive2012/
raFirdousTowerKuwaitCity/tabid/3859/
age/en-GB/Default.aspx.

ncil on Tall Buildings and Urban
t (CTBUH), 'Sowwah Square,
habi', February 2014:. www.ctbuh.
llBuildings/FeaturedTallBuildings/
edTallBuildingArchive2013/
ahSquareAbuDhabi/tabid/6065/language/en-
fault.aspx.

rmation taken from the Skyscraper Center
Council on Tall Buildings and Urban Habitat
JH): www.skyscrapercenter.com (as of
ust 2014).

wall faces into the void and serves as a contrast to the transparent glazed walls that wrap the rest of the building. The openings in the south wall are designed to limit solar penetration. The materiality pays poetic homage to vernacular materials and works to combine the transparency of the new and the solidity of the old.[7]

Goettsch Partners' Al Khatem Tower in Sowwah Square, Abu Dhabi (2013) acknowledges the climate by considering how tall buildings meet the ground. The project is the centrepiece of Al Maryah Island (formerly Sowwah Island) and the city's new sustainably motivated urban framework entitled 'Plan Abu Dhabi 2030'. The stock exchange is elevated and the tower bases are angled and oriented to create a cooler microclimate for pedestrians throughout the landscaped plaza. The building employs an extensive double facade system to protect its active shading system that is projected to save 7,200 kWh of electricity per day across all four towers. The system is designed to respond to the 4°C (40°F) temperature differential across the envelope and protect the building and its occupants from the intense sandstorms and constant corrosive mist of the Gulf environment.[8] As the first mixed-use project in Abu Dhabi to be pre-certified LEED-CS Gold, it is clearly setting a very high bar for future projects in the region.

The Future of Tall Building in the Gulf Region

For a region with an extremely short history in tall building and that has exhibited ambitious dreams and aspirations, the impact of the 2008 global financial crisis was substantial and a number of planned projects remain unbuilt. The combined total of projects on hold, abandoned or classed as visionary for the Gulf is estimated by the CTBUH to be 192, with 121 of these in Dubai alone. Although the region is beginning to recover, only 38 projects that will exceed 200 metres (660 feet) are currently under construction and are targeted for completion by 2019 (the announced completion date for Kingdom Tower in Jeddah).[9]

However, abandoning quickly conceived boom projects might well be to the benefit of the region as it moves into the 21st century. Many recently completed projects demonstrate greater technical proficiency combined with more sensitive approaches to the climate, which may contribute to creating a new tall building vernacular. The adaptation of the double facade system to substitute a shading screen as the exterior element, for instance, seems to be emerging as a climate-specific response on an increasing number of projects. Many projects strongly reference the successful strategies employed in the Sheikh Rashid Tower, the National Commercial Bank and the Al Faisaliyah Tower. This bodes well for the future of the environment and for the future of tall buildings in the region. ᴆ

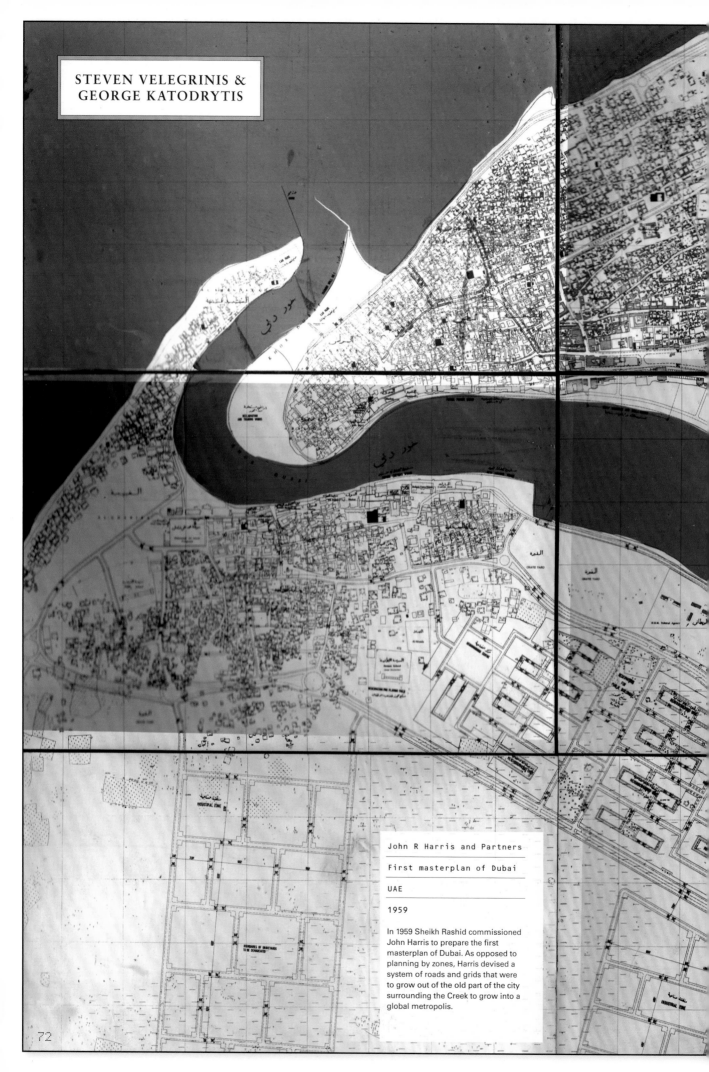

STEVEN VELEGRINIS &
GEORGE KATODRYTIS

John R Harris and Partners

First masterplan of Dubai

UAE

1959

In 1959 Sheikh Rashid commissioned
John Harris to prepare the first
masterplan of Dubai. As opposed to
planning by zones, Harris devised a
system of roads and grids that were
to grow out of the old part of the city
surrounding the Creek to grow into a
global metropolis.

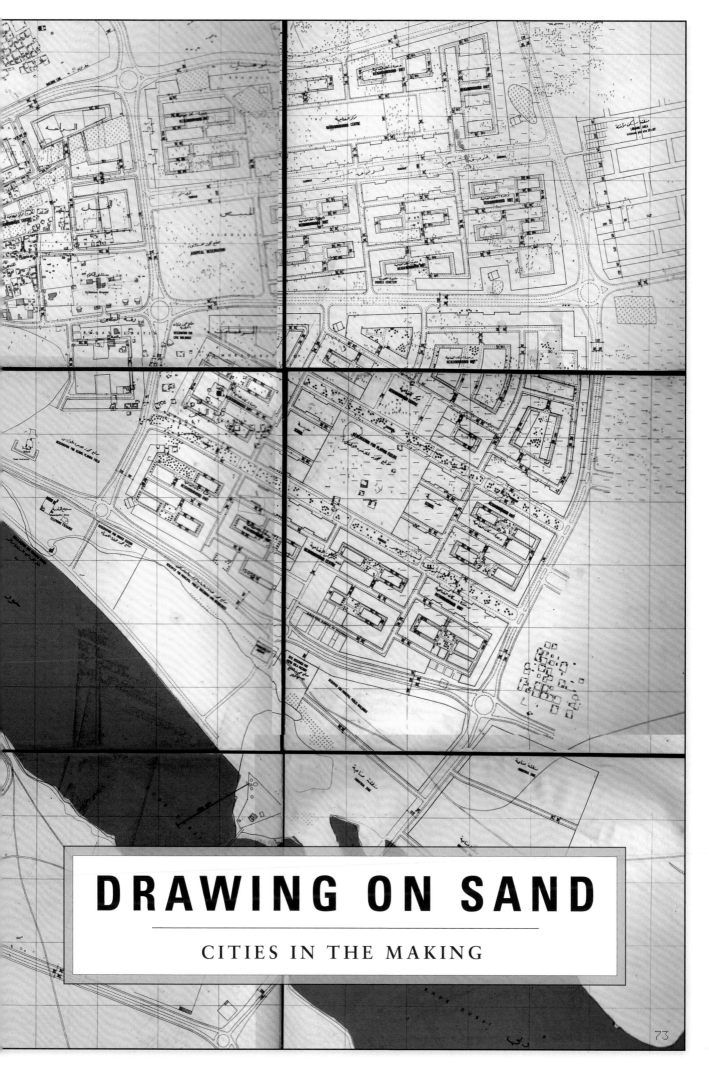

DRAWING ON SAND

CITIES IN THE MAKING

Steven Velegrinis, Director of Urban Design for Perkins+Will in Dubai, and Guest-Editor **George Katodrytis** liken Gulf cities to the shifting sands that they sit upon. Showing urban development to be in a constant state of flux in the region, they highlight four key eras in the unprecedented rapid development of these cities.

Gulf cities, like all urban organisms, act as metabolic fields. They exist in a constant state of flux and, as with the desert sands they are built upon, they can never be regarded as a 'completed' proje They are incipient cities seemingly in a constant state of becomin Since the 1970s the pace and tempo of Gulf urbanism has shocke a world accustomed to slow and considered city/nature dialectics Whereas historically cities evolved over millennia, cities such as Dubai, Doha, Manama and Abu Dhabi sprang up in successive waves of rapid growth as fully formed urban agglomerations. Th article seeks to map out that process through four key eras that describe the evolution of Gulf cities. In doing so it also seeks to n a trajectory for future development.

Act 1

Traditional Communities of the Region in the Pre-Modern E

Most Gulf cities have their origins in antiquity and dependence o the landscape of the region. Traditional Gulf communities were based on tribal systems that governed both nomadic and settled communities.[1] In most cases these tribes belonged to larger grou represented by the sheikhdoms of, for example, the Al Maktoum Dubai, the Al Nayhans in Abu Dhabi, and the Al Thanis in Qata which provided stability and established regional economic ties. These settlements and the tribal landownership system underpin them played a significant role in the later stages of urban development, including during the advent of hydrocarbon econo in the Gulf in the 1960s.

Act 2

Modernist Aspirations from the 1960s to the 1990s

'I personally never saw Sheikh Zayed put pen to paper,' says Joh Elliott, who in 1966 drew up the first masterplan of Abu Dhabi. always used a camel stick and drew in the sand. He had a unique ability to be able to transpose something from his head into the sand. And he instinctively understood scale and adjacency.'[2] In th 1960s there was immense pressure on the rulers of Gulf sheikhde to develop their states and provide opportunities for citizens. The sudden oil wealth had, inevitably, created an early influx of immigrant workers because of the need for major engineering projects. Almost all of the major Gulf states invited foreign architects and engineers to develop masterplans and construct projects on a scale that had not been seen in the region. On one hand, the rulers' visions were forward thinking and courageous; the other, city development has remained tied to its Islamic origi a feat that may often go unnoticed by the casual visitor to the G

The case of the UAE is particularly interesting. The British architect John R Harris produced the masterplan for Dubai in 1959, an extended grid of roads from the Creek out to inhabit th desert. Sir William Halcrow & Partners did the same for Sharjah few years later, introducing trading regions and zones. Abu Dhat established a grid of urban blocks and a connected superblock for small communities. Each emirate had its own plan and the distinctive vision of its local ruler.

In 1958, Sheikh Rashid bin Saeed Al Maktoum became the r of Dubai, and began to envision drastic changes in urban strateg to provide an economic future for its inhabitants. A year later he commissioned Harris as Dubai's first town planner. Harris plann a system of roads and roundabouts throughout the desert on a grid that was to grow out of the old part of the city and beyond

Aerial view of Dubai Creek and Deira

Dubai, UAE

c 1950

Early development along the Creek in Shindagha (foreground), Deira (left) and Bur Dubai (background). In the late 1950s, only small boats could navigate the shallow waterway that was subject to silting. Dredging that began in 1961 opened up possibilities for larger vessels and greater opportunities for trade along the Creek.

surrounding Creek, and provide opportunities for trade via
...structural projects such as the airport and Port Rashid. He
...duced a revised plan in 1971 (see pp 100–5 of this issue)
...made recommendations for building heights and controlled
...ding developments, but was missing the density control,
...ch theoretically encouraged landowners to build entirely over
...r plots without any setback requirements. As a result of this,
...ra and Bur Dubai became dense urban areas with the highest
...ic diversity in the city, which encouraged a mercantile
...nomy. In 1979 Harris completed the Sheikh Rashid Tower
...rld Trade Centre), which established the beginning of Sheikh
...ed Road that was to connect the old town to the new
...elopments of Dubai towards Abu Dhabi.
...At the same time, new laws were introduced in the outskirts,
...iring residential buildings to be set back from plot
...ndaries and marking the end for the inward-looking Arab
...rtyard house, traditionally built around the plot's perimeter.
...n then on, self-contained and air-conditioned family villas
...ld be built behind high boundary walls.
...Given that the early masterplans in the Gulf were essentially
...ted as large engineering and infrastructural projects, it is no
...rise that masterplanning was also a means to accomplish
...a-projects. This was a trend that began in the 1960s and
...inued until the 1990s. Even until 1977, the Planning
...ion of the Dubai Municipality was under the Engineering
...artment, illustrating an approach that focused on
...astructure rather than on the development of an urban fabric.
...need to accommodate waves of immigrants arriving to the
...seeking employment resulted in 'engineering' cities rather
...planning communities.

John R Harris and Partners

Model of the World Trade
Centre

Dubai, UAE

1975

In 1975, Sheikh Rashid commissioned
John Harris to build the Dubai World
Trade Centre. The model shows the early
proposal of an office tower, a hotel and
an exhibition complex.

...dential developments

...i, UAE

...73

...xpansion of residential
...bourhoods in the early 1970s
...s the preference for sprawl
...ensity.

Aerial view of Dubai
Creek and Deira

Dubai, UAE

1990

right: The 1971 'Dubai Development
Plan Review' recognised the
historical and economic importance
of the dense development along the
Creek in the section of Dubai known
as Deira.

Act 3

Aspirations for Hedonistic Modernism in the Gulf, 1990s to 2008

By the 1990s, Gulf cities such as Kuwait, Doha and Manama no lor relied solely on trade. The influx of expatriates and growing number of tourists began unprecedented colonisation of these coastal cities. Urbanism began to evolve into lifestyle hubs, business centres, remo resorts and endless patterns of suburbs. As prosperity increased in th Gulf, these isolated, nomadic structures formed the basis by which t new wealth was distributed in terms of land, use and special legislat

In the post-9/11 investment environment, foreign direct investment found a new home in the Middle East as Dubai sought to attract regional and international capital. Through formation of government-linked companies such as Emaar, Nahkeel and Dubai Properties, investment supported the grand visions of turning Dubai into a spectacle of global proportions. This is best represented by developments such as the Burj Al Arab hotel in 1999 and the man-made Palm Jumeirah islands in 2006. As state-sponsored developers competed for attention, they sought to outdo each other with projec that were increasingly larger and grander. The result was a series of satellite cities-within-cities including Downtown Dubai (previously known as Downtown Burj Dubai), Dubai Marina, the Jumeirah Lakes Towers district, Internet City, Knowledge Village, Media City, International Media Production City, Humanitarian City, Mohamm bin Rashid City, Motor City and Dubai Outlet City.

The hubris and spectacle created by this series of developments gained widespread global attention and revealed a new urban morphology that confounded contemporary theory. This complex se of developments is summarised below according to typology.

Waterfronts and Coastal Resorts

The development of man-made waterfronts and resorts across the region was intended to transform the coastline and thus increase tourism. Perhaps the greatest example of this typology are the Palm Jumeirah islands developed by Nakheel, and other artificial island developments in Dubai that were intended to expand its coastal lan from 45 to over 1,500 kilometres (28 to 930 miles). These include t Palm Deira, Palm Jebel Ali, the World Islands, the Universe and, fina the immense Waterfront City project masterplanned by OMA to accommodate an eventual population of 1.5 million people. Howev with the exception of the Palm Jumeirah, all of them remain largely undeveloped, and some were never realised. The Dubai Marina, designed by HOK and developed by Emaar, was the world's largest planned waterfront community at completion of the first phase in 2003. And where Dubai led, the other Gulf states followed. The Pe Qatar in Doha, the first phase of which was completed in 2012, is a series of artificial islands spanning nearly 4 million square metre (43 million square feet). It is the first land in Qatar to be available for freehold ownership by 45,000 residents, mainly foreign nation In Bahrain, the Durrat Al Bahrain project (due for completion in 2015) is an array of crescent-shaped islands far from the establish urban fabric of Manama. One of the most high-profile developme is Gensler Architects' Saadiyat Cultural District masterplan, Abu Dhabi. This coastal museum-city will be the home of the new Guggenheim by Frank Gehry, the Louvre by Jean Nouvel, and the Zayed National Museum by Foster + Partners.

Sheikh Zayed Road

Dubai, UAE

2013

The 1979 Sheikh Rashid Tower established the beginning of Sheikh Zayed Road to expand Dubai away from the Creek and pointing towards Abu Dhabi and the West.

Gensler Associates

Saadiyat Cultural District masterplan

Abu Dhabi, UAE

due for completion 2018

below: The masterplan will house a new city of 150,000 residents surrounded by major cultural institutions including the Guggenheim and Louvre.

Regeneration

...ond typology that emerged in this period is based on the
...eration of existing urban areas. These primarily concentrated
...storing or re-creating traditional urban environments,
...ould be seen as a reaction against the claims of blatant
...alisation by way of re-enacting a lost – and mainly ambiguous
...ntity. Dubai led these efforts through early restoration projects
...e Bastakiya and Shindaga areas.

...rojects such as Msheireb Downtown Doha (originally named
...t of Doha and due for completion in 2016) (see pp 92–9) and
...Waqif, also in Doha, seek to engage with, preserve, restore
...adaptively reuse the existing urban fabric. The Heart of Doha
...prises one of the world's largest collections of buildings using
...inability principles clustered around the Al Barahat Square,
...other civic space including mixed-use, residential, commercial
...retail buildings. In Sharjah, the Heart of Sharjah conservation
...ct (due for completion in 2025) and Sharjah Lagoons
...erplan by Dar Al-Omran and Green Concepts Landscape
...itects, which began in 2011, are aimed at preserving and
...nnecting the city and the lagoons that served as the heart of the
...city.

...ther projects have sought to re-create the character of the
...acular in urban developments mainly as tourist destinations.
...approach includes the Old Town, Souq Al Bahar and Palace
...l projects in the Downtown Dubai wider area that exploit the
...erplan density and specific language to create a traditional
...ext. Souq Madinat Jumeirah and the surrounding hotel
...plex is another mega-project that employs this approach.

...l Omran and Green
...pts Landscape Architects

...ah Lagoons

...ah, UAE

...or completion 2025

The Sharjah Lagoons masterplan
covers 27 square kilometres (10
square miles) in the urban centre of
Sharjah. It proposes a comprehensive
public open space system to act as a
green infrastructure network.

Desert

In contrast to the other typologies mentioned above, a series of
developments emerged during the same period that sought to
transform unremarkable vast inland areas of desert into spacious
new cities and suburbs. As with the waterfront developments, the
aim was to create appeal, in this case via the stylised suburban
homes of projects such as Dubai's Arabian Ranches and Falconcity
of Wonders, neither of which has been realised, that would appeal to
expatriate families. However, perhaps one of the most well-known
examples is Downtown Dubai, a community that provides the setting
for the world's tallest building, Skidmore, Owing & Merrill's Burj
Khalifa (2010), around a lake and a canal system. Surrounding the
Burj Khalifa district is the Business Bay development designed for a
population of 135,000.

In Saudi Arabia, where the imperative was to create economic
development for a large and growing population, a series of six
metropolises known as the 'economic cities' are currently planned
on undeveloped lands. The King Abdullah City for Atomic and
Renewable Energy (K.A.CARE) near Riyadh, for example, has a total
development area of 180 square kilometres (70 square miles) located
along the Red Sea coast north of Jeddah, and is currently under
construction. These economic cities are intended to help diversify the
oil-based economy of the kingdom by bringing in direct foreign and
domestic investment. In Abu Dhabi, Masdar City designed by Foster
+ Partners is a mixed-use, low-rise, high-density development that
includes the headquarters for the International Renewable Energy
Agency (IRENA) and the recently completed Masdar Institute.

A final subset of the desert typology are the urban projects
in which spectacle revolves around sustainability and vernacular
approaches. The best example of this is Foster + Partners' Masdar
City masterplan (2008). Masdar was designed as the world's first
zero-carbon city and is positioned over 6 square kilometres (2 square
miles) next to Abu Dhabi's International Airport.

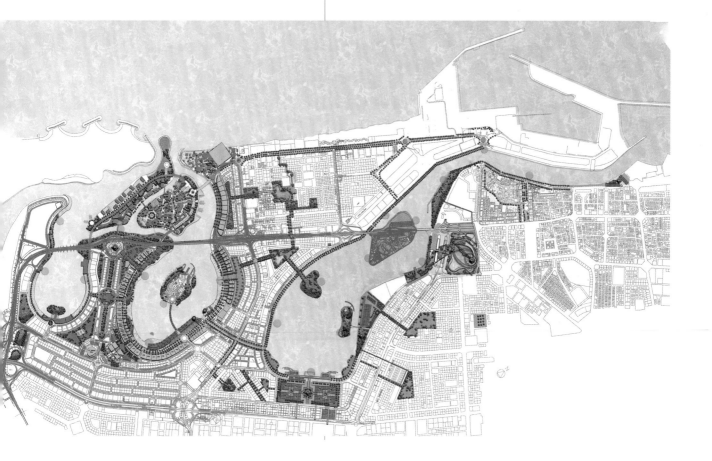

Foster + Partners

Masdar City
masterplan

Abu Dhabi, UAE

2008

The new city relies on solar and other
renewable energy. Masdar City is being
constructed 17 kilometres (11 miles)
east-southeast of Abu Dhabi and hosts the
Masdar Institute and the headquarters of
the International Renewable Energy Agency
(IRENA).

ct 4

n & Bust … and Boom:
ing Forward to Getting it Right

period of extreme optimism leading up to the global financial
of 2008 represents a particular form of urbanism that
oped in the Gulf. However, there were exceptions to this
acle for spectacle's sake and the culture of 'bigger, better, faster'.
cts such as Masdar City paid greater attention to environmental
inability, and Saadiyat Island in Abu Dhabi sought to create
tural district comprised of imported museums and cultural
utions (see pp 26–27). A lengthy hiatus followed, and the
ery in the property market only really commenced in 2012.
atar this recovery was led by optimism following on from the
ssful bid to host the 2022 FIFA World Cup. In the UAE, Dubai's
ssful bid to host the World Expo 2020 had a visible impact as
truction began once again. The intervening period and the flight
vestors away from more speculative development had, however,
amentally changed the market in the Gulf. A market almost
ely composed of speculative investors transformed into one of
ominantly end users who were not seeking superlatives, but
r high-quality products focused on livability, and a public realm
was conducive to outdoor lifestyles.

New projects have sought to provide alternatives to the
lative developments of the past decade. The Dubai Design
ict (d3), developed by Woods Bagot and currently under
truction, attempts to capitalise on the Gulf's and Dubai's status
ghest per-capita consumers of luxury and designer goods. With
itious sustainability goals, the project is developed around a
ework of generous landscapes and anchored by hybridised
land to appeal as a lifestyle destination. The multi-use City
k project in Dubai, re-masterplanned by Perkins+Will in 2014
se one architecture by Benoy Architects and Dewan Architects
ngineers was completed in 2011), was conceptualised as a
ively low-rise and predominantly outdoor environment. Located
ne site of an abandoned mega-project, the developer, Meraas,
focused on the idea of lifestyle-oriented development in the Gulf.
Beach project, also by Meraas, with its series of pavilion-like
ctures, also typifies a renewed focus on outdoor environments.
similar vein, the Urban Planning Council (UPC) of Abu Dhabi,
blished in 2007, has shown an increasing bias towards qualitative
more modest development with the introduction of its revised
ic Realm Design Manual and the first Open Space Masterplan
he Plan Abu Dhabi 2030. Reinforcing the move away from
itious growth, the UPC also commissioned Arup to revise its
2030 for Abu Dhabi, and this has resulted in a reduction in
vth objectives to more modest levels (albeit still very rapid for
established city).

The Gulf cities continue to grow into emerging complex urban
ropolises. The projects outlined here suggest another phase of
lopment currently underway, where ambitious plans are realised,
in a manner that is far more qualitative and focused on future
bitants. Unlike in Europe, the Gulf city never seems to become
rated. The abundance of empty land and endless waterfronts
inue to provide opportunities for new developments. And at
same time, the early downtown projects of the 1970s and 1980s
being transformed and regenerated. These cities, like all urban
nisms, are truly metabolic fields. ⚙

Woods Bagot

Dubai Design District (d3)

phase 1

Dubai, UAE

2014

The 220-hectare (540-acre) d3 masterplan
is adjacent to Dubai's new downtown. It
proposes a live, work, play community
developed around a landscape
framework and anchored by hybridised
parkland and a 2-kilometre (1.2-mile)
public waterfront.

*The Gulf cities continue to
grow into emerging complex
urban metropolises. The
projects outlined here suggest
another phase of development
currently underway, where
ambitious plans are realised,
but in a manner that is far more
qualitative and focused on
future inhabitants.*

Notes
1. Frauke Heard-Bey, 'The Tribal Society of
the UAE and its Traditional Economy', in
Ibrahim Al Abed and Peter Hellyer (eds),
United Arab Emirates: A New Perspective,
Trident Press (London), 2001, p 98.
2. Ann Wimsatt, 'The Houses that John
Built', *The National*, 27 November 2010:
www.thenational.ae/arts-culture/the-
houses-that-john-built.

Kelly Hutzell, Rami el Samahy and Adam Himes

Two Eras of Planning in Doha, Qatar

Inexha
Amb

*Architects and researchers in urban design,
Kelly Hutzell, Rami el Samahy and Adam Himes, reflect on
how the present structure of Doha in Qatar is a result of
intermittent state interventions – failures as well as successes.
They explain how these sporadic initiatives manifested
themselves in two main bursts of activity:
1971–86 and 1999 to the present day.*

Kristina Ricco/4dDoha,
Map of the Qatar Peninsula,
4 July 1937
School of Architecture,
Carnegie Mellon University,
Pittsburgh, Pennsylvania,
2014

Part of the 4dDoha ongoing research project and
based on a map hand-drawn by an anonymous
British diplomat, eight villages are noted as having
merged to form the town of 'Dohah'.

> In spite of its early promise, its frequent bravery, urbanism has been unable to invent and implement at the scale demanded by its apocalyptic demographics.

Rem Koolhaas,
'Whatever Happened
to Urbanism?',
S,M,L,XL, 1995[1]

Twenty years ago, Rem Koolhaas identified a major failure of modern planning as its inability to predict and accommodate the massive population boom of the past century. He was specifically referring to the megacities of Asia and Africa, which are often challenged by limited resources and swelling populations driven largely by rural-to-urban migration. Although these particular factors do not apply to planning in the nations of the Gulf Cooperation Council (GCC), there are parallels nonetheless. In Qatar, and its capital, Doha, there is a particularly marked disjuncture between ambitions (as represented by masterplanning efforts) and reality (as represented by an analysis of the city structure and development). Doha's present structure results from planning's successes and failures, a reflection of sporadic state initiatives.

From modest origins as a cluster of eight villages around a small fortress, Doha has grown dramatically through two major expansions, each fuelled by new revenue streams. In the 1970s, the rise of oil prices allowed the newly independent state to embark on a modern nation-building project, while the exploitation of natural gas in the 2000s has given rise to a second era of state-led construction, this time on an altogether different scale (it is no coincidence that the relative lull that punctuated these two episodes is characterised by a drop in oil prices in the early 1980s). This essay will examine these two eras with a particular focus on the area known originally as New Doha, and today as West Bay or Al Dafna, as a means of gauging the distance between planning and reality.

Episode One: 1971–86

Prior to Qatar's independence in 1971, planning authority was highly fragmented among no fewer than 10 ministries and the office of the Emir. an effort to address rapid population growth and consolidate authority, the Ministry of Municipal Affairs – then responsible chiefly for building regulations and landscaping – hired British architecture and planning offi of Llewelyn-Davies, Weeks, Forestier-Walker & Bor (hereafter 'Llewelyn-Davies') to develop the country's first comprehensive masterplan.[2] The four subsequent masterplans of this era, developed by William L Pereira Associates (WLPA), Shankland Cox Partnership (SCP), Hellmuth, Obata & Kassabaum (HOK) and Dar Al-Handa: Consultants, each built on and were structured by this framework.

What began in 1972 as a modest 'town planning' assignment was radically transformed the following y by a surge in oil prices into fully-fled nation building. New capital projects included buildings for each ministry, port facilities, an airport, a hospital a an iconic restaurant and observation tower. The state also raised the idea of infilling Doha's West Bay to create cache of government-owned land for controlled development.

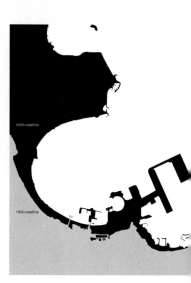

Kristina Ricco/4dDoha,
The changing coastline of Doha,
1956 and 2009,
School of Architecture,
Carnegie Mellon University,
Pittsburgh, Pennsylvania,
2014

Doha's coastline, or Corniche, is paradoxically the city's most defining feature and the one most often and most substantially changed.

Adam Himes and
Kristina Ricco/4dDoha,
'New Doha' as envisioned
by William L Pereira Associates
in 1975, and West Bay in 2014,
School of Architecture,
Carnegie Mellon University,
Pittsburgh, Pennsylvania,
2014

The proposal for a bayside pedestrian greenway peppered with government buildings and in support of high-density neighbourhoods on the headland has given way to a menagerie of fantastical towers and a smattering of villa housing with little regard for pedestrian accessibility.

What began in 1972 as a modest 'town planning' assignment was radically transformed the following year by a surge in oil prices into fully-fledged nation building.

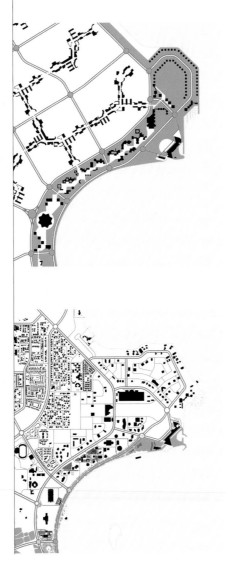

Llewelyn-Davies's original vision of a high-end residential and diplomatic area anchored by a hotel and conference centre was greatly enhanced by the introduction of WLPA in 1975 into 'New Doha': the terminus of the Corniche, a vital link to Qatar University and proposed home to 60,000 residents. WLPA extrapolated this figure from Llewelyn-Davies's population projections made only three years earlier, yet felt compelled to note that 'circumstances in Qatar have changed drastically' and 'it can be assumed that the population of Doha will grow more rapidly, as a result of immigration, than originally anticipated'.[3] The degree to which this underestimated reality is staggering: by 1992 – the final year projected – the actual population of Qatar more than doubled the estimates.[4] SCP released revised estimates in 1981, but fared little better; expecting the population to double by 2000, instead it more than tripled.[5] Linking population growth to immigration and thus, the economy, Dar Al-Handasah's final update in 1985 – early into a prolonged economic downturn – reduced SCP's estimates, further skewing projections.[6]

Despite the population boom, West Bay did not turn into a dense residential community. WLPA completed the Sheraton Hotel and Conference Centre in 1982 and numerous embassies have since opened nearby, but only low-density neighbourhoods were built on the western edge of the reclaimed area. Tree-lined streets planned for the headland were replaced by a forest of towers; on the site of the golf course they were to surround, stands City Centre Mall. Commerce boomed along the newly completed Corniche, leaving the historical centre to stagnate.

Llewelyn-Davies had recommended regenerating Doha's existing core around Souq Waqif as the city's primary hub, devising the method by which the state would purchase property and relocate residents to make way for demolition and redevelopment. Despite extensive demolition, the city lacked a detailed plan for replacement until Dar Al-Handasah submitted proposals in 1985–6, by which time the contracting economy precluded implementation. Early plans envisioned a ceremonial avenue leading from the airport through the area, culminating in the conjoined hyperbolic paraboloids of WLPA's Doha Tower on a peninsula jutting into the bay. Sagging oil prices and competition from West Bay resulted in Grand Hamad Street: an outsized boulevard rending the historical city in two and bordered largely by vacant land for decades.

The failure of the 1976 international competition to develop the Corniche into a ministerial complex left Doha without a cohesive urban strategy to join its two centres.[7] In their 1983 Landscape Master Plan, HOK built on SCP's schematic proposal for pedestrian movement across the historical areas, devising a network of greenways and pedestrian bridges to link open spaces, but did not address West Bay. Planning efforts for the two centres had become divorced from one another, with Dar Al-Handasah detailing old Doha's revival and WLPA expanding their own design for New Doha until 1986. Stagnant oil prices inhibited implementation of either, and further planning efforts were suspended for nearly a decade.

The Architects Collaborative

James Stirling and Partner

Behnisch & Partner

Adam Himes/4dDoha,
The ambition and reality of
Grand Hamad Street, Doha:
1981, existing (top); 1981,
proposed (middle); present
condition (bottom), School of
Architecture, Carnegie Mellon
University, Pittsburgh,
Pennsylvania, 2014

The dense, largely residential urban fabric of pre-modern Doha's historic core was obliterated in favour of a grandiose commercial boulevard, itself abandoned before full realisation.

Adam Himes/4dDoha,
Four visions for Doha's
Government Centre, 1976,
School of Architecture,
Carnegie Mellon University,
Pittsburgh, Pennsylvania,
2014

Ever since the failure to implement Kenzo Tange's winning proposal, Doha has struggled to create a fitting centrepiece to its Corniche.

ode Two: 1999–Present

￼h Hamad bin Khalifa Al Thani's
￼mption of power in 1995 coincided
￼a new surge in the price of oil and,
￼icantly, in the development of new
￼nologies that facilitated the extraction
￼transportation of natural gas, an
￼dant resource for the emirate. This
￼oination allowed the new leader (and
￼ 2013, his son, Sheikh Tamim bin
￼ad Al Thani) to expand the ambitions
￼rlier generations. During this era,
￼terplanning exercises resumed,
￼with the Louis Berger International/
￼framework plan of 1994–7, followed
￼e HOK plan of the early 2000s, and
￼ recently the national masterplan.
￼ever, these plans were superseded by
￼aprojects and massive infrastructural
￼tives, the former encouraging an
￼nism of monocultural enclaves
￼cation City, the Industrial Sector,
￼val City, etc), and the latter providing
￼high-speed connections between them.
￼or the past several years, a group of
￼gn consultants[8] has been developing
￼tional masterplan for the Ministry for
￼icipal Affairs and Urban Planning, and
￼recently released a draft of the Qatar
￼onal Development Framework 2010–
￼ (QNDF). The QNDF identifies several
￼egic planning objectives including
￼evelopment of three centres within
￼capital area (Downtown Doha, West
￼ and the new airport); high-density,
￼sit-oriented developments elsewhere;
￼ngthened and well-integrated public
￼sportation options; and an urban
￼vth boundary around the capital region.
￼ough its scope covers all of Qatar, the
￼ of the framework efforts have been
￼cted where the vast majority lives:
￼ropolitan Doha.[9]

￼At the same time the country's
￼ulation continues to grow dramatically,
￼re projections continue to be
￼erestimated. In 1997, the population
￼sured 522,000; by 2009 it was estimated
￼553,000; as of the end of April 2014 it
￼risen to 2,155,446.[10] QNDF projections
￼mate the population will reach 2.3
￼ion in 2032.[11] Although the final
￼ument has yet to be made public, it is
￼ady out of date.

> ## [...] the country's population continues to grow dramatically, future projections continue to be underestimated.

Kelly Hutzell and Rami el
Samahy/4dDoha,
Spatial strategy concept
for Doha, 2032,
School of Architecture,
Carnegie Mellon University,
Pittsburgh, Pennsylvania,
2014

The Qatar National Development Framework calls
for the reinvigoration of Doha as a multi-nodal city to
ease pressure off of the overburdened Corniche and
diversify the surrounding sprawl.

Kristina Ricco & Blake Lam/4dDoha,
The growth of metropolitan Doha
and its population, 1910-2030,
School of Architecture, Carnegie Mellon University,
Pittsburgh, Pennsylvania,
2014

Little more than a fishing village as recently as the 1950s, Doha has
defied all attempts to predict its growth and today is home to more
than two million people.

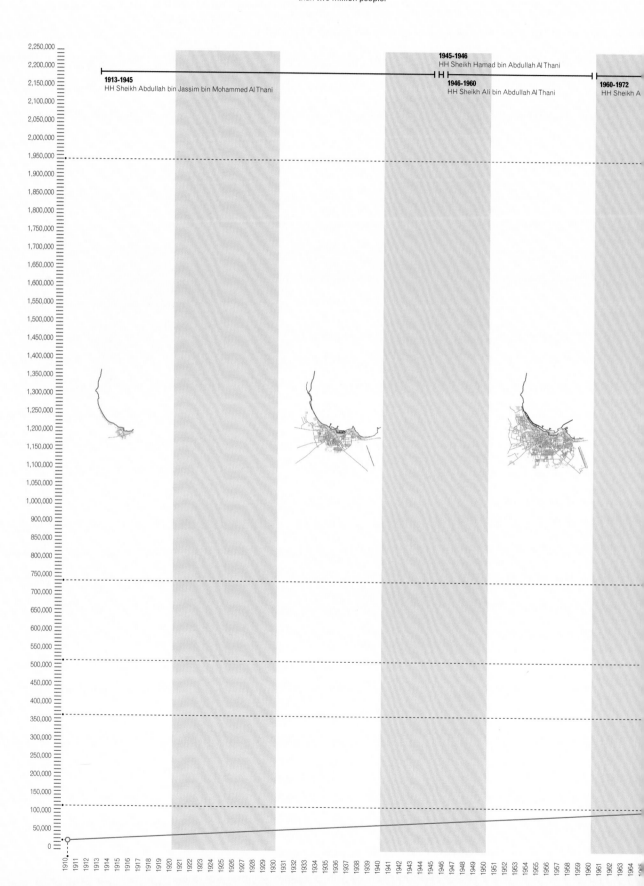

1913-1945
HH Sheikh Abdullah bin Jassim bin Mohammed Al Thani

1945-1946
HH Sheikh Hamad bin Abdullah Al Thani

1946-1960
HH Sheikh Ali bin Abdullah Al Thani

1960-1972
HH Sheikh A

2,400,000
Expected popluation by 2030

1,951,591
Current population

1,275,971
Economically active population

1,201,884
Economically active expatriate population

Khalifa bin Hamad bin Abdullah Al Thani

1995-
HH Sheikh Hamad bin Khalifa Al Thani

505,816
Economically active expatriate population
engaged in the construction sector

1976 1977 1978 1979 1980 1981 1982 1983 1984 1985 1986 1987 1988 1989 1990 1991 1992 1993 1994 1995 1996 1997 1998 1999 2000 2001 2002 2003 2004 2005 2006 2007 2008 2009 2010 2011 2012 2013 2014 2015 2016 2017 2018 2019 2020 2021 2022 2023 2024 2025 2026 2027 2028 2029 2030

*Population information from the Qatar Statistics Authority, Census 2010
and the CIA World Factbook, accessed 16 January 2013.*

This growth is expected to be accommodated by megaprojects currently underway, including Qatari Diar's Lusail City, Barwa's Al Baraha and Msheireb Properties' eponymous project. At 3,500 hectares (8,650 acres), Lusail is an instant city for over 200,000 immediately abutting Doha to the north, and catering to professionals in the oil and gas industries who want to live and work in proximity to Ras Laffan Industrial City. Southwest of the sprawling metropolis lies Al Baraha, which provides both the largest workers' camp in the region (for 53,000 low-income workers) and the largest truck park in the world (4,200 trucks capacity).[12] The Msheireb project aims to regenerate Qatar's social and economic vitality in the restored heart of the congested city centre. From its location, to its studied massing strategy and refined material palette, this mixed-use project for 27,600 represents a marked difference in approach to most others in the region.

Doha's outward expansion has been encouraged by its infrastructure of ring roads and radial spokes, aided by a policy of land acquisition in the centre and land granting on the edges. In the past decade, this road system has been systematically expanded, replacing roundabouts with traffic lights and widening streets with more lanes, all in an effort to accommodate burgeoning traffic. In addition, the upgrading of highways that connect various suburban towns to Doha now make it possible to live further from the centre. As a result, the sprawl of metropolitan Doha is roughly the size of New York City's five boroughs, for a population roughly one-fifth the size.

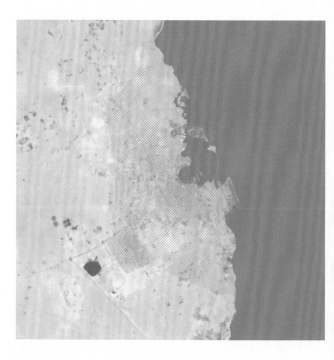

Kristina Ricco/4dDoha,
Land areas of metropolitan Doha
and New York City, 2014,
School of Architecture,
Carnegie Mellon University,
Pittsburgh, Pennsylvania
2014

Rampant sprawl has run far ahead of even Doha's booming population; New York City houses five times as many people in the same area.

Megaproject

Infrastructure Project

Metro

Lusail City

Sharq Crossing

Msheireb

Hamad International Airport

Barwa Al Baraha

New Port Project

Kristina Ricco/4dDoha,
Current megaprojects and
infrastructure developments, Doha, 2014,
School of Architecture,
Carnegie Mellon University,
Pittsburgh, Pennsylvania,
2014

Doha's infrastructural projects promise to make it more accessible
for residents and the global community while massive new developments seek
to stay one step ahead of the city's ever-booming population.

Leading up to the football World Cup in 2022, a number of infrastructure improvements aim to further facilitate urban expansion, with $12.3 billion proposed for road construction alone.[13] Other major projects include an underground metro system, the relocation of the Doha port, the new Hamad International Airport and Sharq Crossing, an ambitious causeway from the new airport to West Bay, together estimated to cost more than $63 billion.[14] Perhaps the best side effect of hosting the World Cup, the Doha Metro light-rail effort has been ramped up in anticipation of the event, with 60 per cent of the final network – 151 kilometres (94 miles) of line and 48 stations – to be completed by 2022. The New Port Project will raise container capacity from 350,000 twenty-foot equivalent units (TEU) in 2010 to 2 million by 2016, thereby alleviating the current delivery bottleneck.[15] Hamad International will handle over 50 million passengers and 2 million tons of cargo per year, making it one of the world's largest airports. Sharq Crossing is a combination of bridges and tunnels designed by Santiago Calatrava that will connect the new airport with West Bay and points to the north of the city.

The professionals of the city are like chess players who lose to computers. A perverse automatic pilot constantly outwits all attempts at capturing the city, exhausts all ambitions of its definition, ridicules the most passionate assertions of its present failure and future impossibility, steers it implacably further on its flight forward.

Rem Koolhaas,
'Whatever Happened to Urbanism?'
S,M,L,XL, 1995[16]

Kristina Ricco/4dDoha,
West Bay, Doha, 2014

Doha's business district, anchored by City Center Mall, is a far cry from the dense, pedestrianised, green residential area originally proposed.

The impact of Sharq Crossing on West Bay is unclear. As a sign that the city has arrived, the neighbourhood is an impressive collection of towers, a few of them even well designed. As a place for working, living and playing, West Bay is at best a work in progress: parking shortages lead to cars parked everywhere, interrupted sidewalks impede pedestrian access, tower bases have little relation to the street, and there are no activated edges whatsoever. In fact, West Bay today represents a mix of well-intended planning overridden by reality, guilty not only of underestimating population growth, but also of failing to address the complexities of implementation, even within a centralised structure.

Twenty years ago, Koolhaas predicted the demise of urbanism as defined by 20th-century practice. While correctly identifying urbanism's key failure as an inability to handle the population explosion, he was wrong in anticipating its downfall. In fact, much of the profession continues to practise urbanism in the 20th-century mode, essentially unchanged.

On the landward side of Hamad International is Doha's planned third centre, according to the QNDF; ironically, it is Rem Koolhaas's Office for Metropolitan Architecture (OMA) that has won the commission to masterplan the project. It takes the form of a series of four rings, reminiscent of crop circles, and arranged in a line parallel to the new airport. The project proposes 10 square kilometres (4 square miles) of commercial, retail, hotel and residential programme that connects the city to the airport, with an anticipated capacity of 200,000 people. According to OMA's website, it is expected that phase one will be 'mostly complete' by 2022.[17] Even Rem, it would appear, is unable to resist the promise of false certainty offered by a masterplan. ∆

Notes

1. Rem Koolhaas, 'Whatever Happened to Urbanism?', in OMA, Rem Koolhaas and Bruce Mau, *S,M,L,XL*, Monacelli Press (New York), 1995, p 961.

2. A number of other consultants were hired at this time with expertise in economics, social anthropology and urban planning, among other fields. While Llewelyn-Davies was chief among them in producing a comprehensive plan, also worthy of note is the traffic-engineering consultancy Peat, Marwick, Mitchell and Company. For a firs-thand account of post-independence-era planning, see John Lockerbie, 'Planning in Qatar 01', Catnaps.org: http://catnaps.org/islamic/planning.html.

3. William L Pereira Associates, *New Doha Planning Studies, Volume One: Concept Plan*, William L Pereira Associates (Los Angeles), 1975, pp 33–4.

4. Note that this is a comparison of the national population, though in 1977 Doha accounted for nearly 80 per cent of Qatar's population. See *ibid*, p 33, and United States Census Bureau, 'International Programs – Country Rankings', 2014: www.census.gov/population/international/data/countryrank/rank.php.

5. These figures describe the population of metropolitan Doha, including Al Rayyan. See Shankland Cox Partnership, *Qatar Planning Studies, Summary Report*, The State of Qatar, Ministry of Municipal Affairs (Doha), 1981, p 7, and The State of Qatar, The Planning Council, The Secretariat General Statistics Department, *The General Population and Housing Census 2004*, The State of Qatar, The Planning Council, The Secretariat General Statistics Department (Doha), 2004, p 47.

6. Dar Al-Handasah Consultants (Shair & Partners), *Doha Inner City Redevelopment, Draft Report No 2: Master Plan*, Dar Al-Handasah Consultants (Doha), 1985, pp 9 and 53.

7. The offices of Kenzo Tange, James Stirling, The Architects Collaborative and Günter Behnisch each submitted megastructural complexes for the sweep of land between the Diwan Al Amiri and West Bay. Tange's proposal was selected, but unrealised, as in the time it took to hold the competition and declare a winner, a number of ministries had already moved ahead with the construction of separate buildings of their own design.

8. A large number of consultants appear to be involved, including Oriental Consultants, PCBK, Surbana and Place Dynamix.

9. Agatino Rizzo, 'Rapid Urban Development and National Master Planning in Arab Gulf countries: Qatar as a case study', *Cities*, 39, 2014, pp 50–7.

10. Ministry of Development Planning and Statistics: www.qsa.gov.qa/eng/PopulationStructure.htm.

11. Sindu Nair, 'Future Forward', *Qatar Today*, December 2010, p 35. Nair quotes figures provided by Ian Lynne, then principal of Place Dynamix and the project manager of the Qatar National Master Plan.

12. 'Barwa Al Baraha Construction Enters New Phase', *Gulf Times*, 5 May 2014: www.gulf-times.com/qatar/178/details/390912/barwa-al-baraha-construction-enters-new-phase.

13. Gavin Davis, 'Qatar Announces $26bn Plan to Develop Highway and Sewage Network', *The Big Project*, 13 January 2014: www.bigprojectme.com/news/qatar-announces-26bn-plan-to-develop-highway-and-sewage-network/.

14. MEED, 'Qatar Projects 2014': http://entosektos.gr/wp-content/uploads/2014/04/MEED_Qatar_Projects_Analysis.pdf.

15. Martin Ashcroft and Jon Bradley, 'A Greenfield Port', *Business Excellence Weekly*, 13 January 2013: www.npp.com.qa/Business%20Excellence%20Magazine.pdf.

16. OMA, Rem Koolhaas and Bruce Mau, *op cit*, pp 961–3.

17. OMA, HIA Airport City, Qatar, Doha, 2013: http://oma.eu/projects/2013/hia-airport-city/.

Msheireb Properties

Msheireb Downtown Doha

Doha, Qatar

due for completion 2016

Map showing the central location
of Msheireb Downtown Doha.

Varkki Pallathucheril

Doha in Qatar and Sharjah
in the UAE are both
currently looking to their
own heritage for inspiration
in the redevelopment of
their urban cores or hearts.
Varkki Pallathucheril, an
expert in urban planning
and Professor at the College
of Architecture, Art and
Design at the American
University of Sharjah
(AUS), considers the impact
challenges of this type of
development.

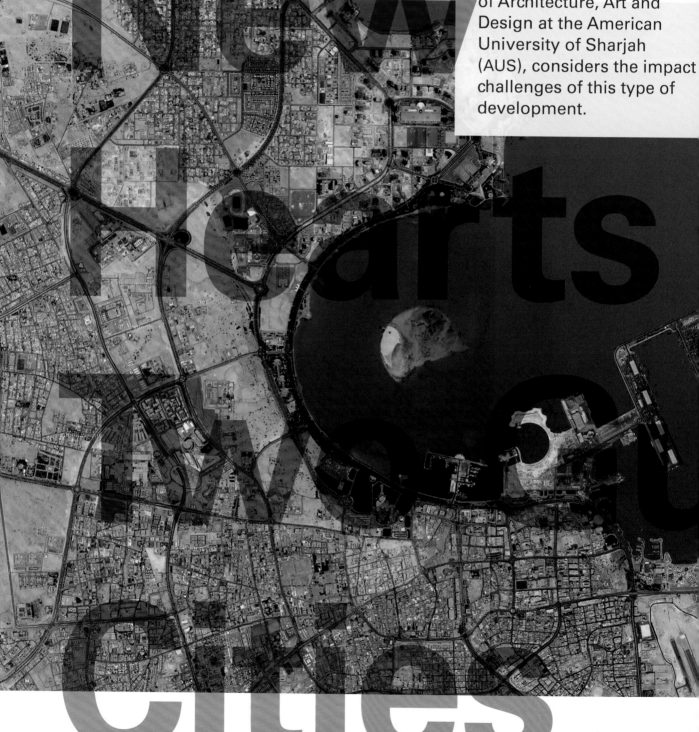

Gulf cites – Doha in Qatar, and Sharjah in the UAE – are
enting and remaking the urban fabric that lies at each
eir hearts. Rather than transplanting urban forms from
here, as is the case in urban development projects across
ulf, these two cities are looking to their own heritage for
ation. While laudable, these efforts are not without their
enges.

n Dynamics

y of today's gleaming Gulf cities had their roots in humble
i where the urban fabric responded to local climatic
itions, social norms and locally available construction
rials.[1] In this fabric, a few masonry structures housed
utions and the social elite; most other structures were
ed with palm frond, animal skin or both. In general, homes
inward looking to protect the privacy of the household.
roximity of buildings resulted in narrow shaded paths that
ed people to move around, primarily on foot, in comfort.
organic fabric of these nuclei reflected the accretion of
ordinated changes – additions, alterations and demolitions
r time, and became the heart of the city.
he discovery of oil and the dramatic economic expansion
was triggered starting in the 1970s transformed the physical
c and the social structure of Gulf cities as expatriate
ers flocked to take up newly created jobs. Citizens were
l vacant land then on the periphery, which was used for
r homes with modern amenities such as air conditioning.
triates in need of housing rented the homes vacated by
itizens. Market forces drove demolition of many of these
tures that were then replaced by new multistoried buildings
tructed out of concrete and masonry, which projected
hage of progress commensurate with the new wealth.
once-organic fabric was significantly re-engineered, in
cular to accommodate cars. As a result, the Gulf city was
ly rendered unrecognisable to those who witnessed the
formation.
y the turn of the 21st century, the hearts of these cities no
er appeared healthy. The housing stock had been rented
aves of successively poorer expatriates, culminating in
pancy by groups of low-wage male labourers. Similarly,
l establishments that occupied spaces on the ground floors
sidential buildings were increasingly more humble as high-
establishments located in newly developed areas. With lower
, property owners invested less in maintenance and the built
onment appeared worn out, neglected and unsightly.
ut these apparently wilting places still served a vital
ose. They provided housing that low-wage workers – the
stay of the Gulf economies – could afford. Affordable
ing was in short supply as real-estate developers focused on
ts from housing the better-off. As Herbert Gans discovered
des ago in the US, areas that seem visually blighted
rtheless have strong social networks.[2] Likewise, expatriates
g in the hearts of Gulf cities formed networks based on
ed family, ethnicity and national origin that provided
ficant social support for those separated from their families
to economic migration. Furthermore, these areas hosted
amer yet resilient economic networks delivering specialised
ls and services, for example inexpensive custom tailoring not
able elsewhere in the city.

Morphology of Old Town
Ras al Khaimah (top)

the Heart of Sharjah
(centre)

Msheireb Downtown Doha
(bottom)

The Heart of Sharjah and Msheireb
Downtown Doha projects seek
to re-create the historical urban
fabric, but with a coarser grain that
has longer linear spaces and fewer
changes in direction.

Allies and Morrison,
Arup and AECOM

Msheireb Downtown Doha

Doha, Qatar

due for completion 2016

Rendering of a public space from
the masterplan for Msheireb
Downtown Doha. The space is
intended to be lined by hotels,
retail and food outlets, and the
entrance to a Metro station. This
is one of two public spaces in the
project of a scale greater than
those typically encountered in
historical places of the Gulf.

Bird's-eye view of Msheireb
Downtown Doha. The project
appears to re-create the organic
street network typical of historical
urban places of the Gulf.

since this value was largely invisible, however, the hearts
[of] ulf cities suffered in visual comparisons with their newer
[nei]hbourhoods. To exacerbate the problem, the degraded
[a]res occupied highly symbolic locations associated with the
[citie]s' origins and could be considered inappropriate. Ultimately,
[how]ever, economic forces rang the death knell as these areas did
[not] represent the best return in terms of revenue generation.

[New] Hearts

[Both] Doha and Sharjah have launched real-estate redevelopment
[proj]ects to realise their visions for a new, tradition-inspired
[urba]n fabric. Msheireb Downtown Doha (originally named
[Hear]t of Doha), developed by Doha-based Msheireb Properties,
[is in]tended to 'regenerate and preserve the historical heart
[of D]oha' and to 'revive the old commercial district with a
[new] architectural language that is modern, yet inspired by
[trad]itional Qatari heritage and architecture'.[3] The Heart of
[Shar]jah project, developed by the Sharjah Investment and
[Dev]elopment Authority, seeks to 'restore and revamp the city's
[trad]itional areas to create a tourist and trade destination with
[cont]emporary artistic touches, yet retain the feel of the 1950s'.[4]

[The] Msheireb Downtown is on a 31-hectare (77-acre) site, about
[500] metres (1,640 feet) away from Doha's waterfront, bounded
[on a]ll sides by major traffic arteries. Immediately to the north
[is th]e Diwan Al Amiri complex, the seat of Qatari political
[pow]er. To the west lies Souq Waqif, historically the commercial
[and] social centre of Doha, now reconstructed as a pedestrian
[stre]et with retail and hospitality establishments.[5] Four historical
[stru]ctures remain after the area was razed for redevelopment:
[thre]e houses that belonged to leading Qatari families and one
[that] belonged to the Shell Company.[6] Master development
[cons]ultants are Arup, EDAW (now AECOM), and Allies and
[Mo]rrison working in collaboration, and diverse firms have
[prov]ided design services.[7]

[The] Heart of Sharjah is located along a channel that
[conn]ects an inland body of water, the Khalid Lagoon, with the
[gul]f. Wooden dhows carrying goods between Sharjah and Iran
[wou]ld, until recently, moor along the banks of this channel.
[The] dhows, and the human activity they generated, have since
[been] relocated to the opposite shore. The area has remnants
[of a] linear souk (shopping area) and a number of structures
[that] re-create the vernacular architecture of the region and
[hou]se cultural and artistic activities (museums, galleries and a
[thea]tre). The Sharjah Biennial, a major art event that is gaining
[wor]ldwide recognition, is held in this area. The most recent
[bien]nial in 2013 saw the insertion of new exhibition spaces
[desi]gned by Mona El Mousfy that received critical acclaim for
[dep]arting in engaging ways from their 'historicist' surroundings.[8]
[Whi]le no public record of the current planners and designers
[of th]e project can be found, the Jordanian firm Dar Al-Omran
[prod]uced an early scheme.[9]

[As] As mentioned at the outset, both redevelopment projects
[serio]usly consider historical precedent. Supported by the
[Qat]ar Foundation, a consortium of consultants for Msheireb
[Dow]ntown Doha scrutinised precedents from the country's
[histo]rical urban fabric: neighbourhood (fereej); alleyway
[(sik]ka); open space (baraha); and reception room (majlis).[10]
[The] consultants considered how climate might drive an urban
[desig]n that supports walking (for example, a shaded public realm

Proposed *sikka* (alley) between heritage houses and institutional buildings (the Guards building and the National Archive) in Msheireb Downtown Doha.

Proposed *sikka* (alley) in a private *fereej* (neighbourhood) of townhouse clusters in Msheireb Downtown Doha.

Allies and Morrison and
Burns & McDonnell

Msheireb Downtown Doha

Doha, Qatar

due for completion 2016

Entrance courtyard to an
institutional building in Msheireb
Downtown Doha. Vertical surfaces
that ring the courtyard have
several openings that activate
the space.

paths oriented to channel breezes). The analysis contrasted
traditional building footprint, which covered the entire site
provided open space within, with its inverse: structures
rounded by open space. Anne Coles and Peter Jackson have
ilarly documented the built heritage of the UAE.[11] The Heart
harjah project refers more explicitly to precedents of urban
m, public realm and architectural features.

When viewed as figure-ground diagrams, both redevelopment
jects can be seen as attempting to re-create the organic
work of narrow shaded paths and intense small-scale public
ces that once characterised settlements along the coast of
Gulf. Both seek to privilege pedestrian movement, which in
heireb Downtown is accomplished by restricting vehicular
fic to streets below grade. The Heart of Sharjah targets
ure- and tourism-related combinations of institutional, retail
hospitality uses, while Msheireb Downtown more generally
es office, retail, hospitality and residential uses. Msheireb
wntown incorporates taller mid-rise structures that result in
ter density than in the Heart of Sharjah.

nplex Challenges

h projects take an approach to the built environment that is
elcome change from contemporary real-estate development
tures in the Gulf; however, a challenge fundamental to the
gn of the public realm in Arab-Islamic cities, well illustrated
pair of renderings of Msheireb Downtown,[12] remains
esolved. The conundrum is this: How to reconcile the inward
ntation of buildings with an active, vibrant public realm?
rendering by Allies and Morrison presents a more literal
ifestation of the traditional *sikka*. The vertical surfaces
g the *sikka* present long blank walls uninterrupted by
hing to engage the senses; there is little to activate the space.
rendering by Mossessian & Partners, on the other hand,
cts a *sikka* where the public realm is activated by making
ical surfaces transparent, but the buildings are no longer
ard looking.

Are these two intentions irreconcilable? How were they
uccessfully reconciled in the traditional fabric of Gulf
ements? As Shaima Al Harmoudi has demonstrated, the
n fabric historically had a much finer grain than in the
emporary built environment.[13] As a result, the linear spaces
etween buildings were shorter in length than in today's
velopment projects where real-estate feasibility demands
er block sizes. Shorter lengths and more frequent changes
rection created variety and sustained interest. Also, vertical
aces were more frequently punctuated by doors and other
nings, but openings on opposite sides of these narrow public
es rarely faced each other. In any case, an inward orientation
have been less of an issue because neighbourhoods were
ogeneous with respect to familial and tribal kinship.

n one respect, Msheireb Downtown is more ambitious
the Heart of Sharjah. The Doha project seeks to reverse
nd that has impacted all Gulf cities, namely the move by
ens to homes in increasingly sprawling suburban locations.
le most commendable and desirable on a number of levels,
ing these families back to dense urban settings presents
ficant challenges, not the least of which is the deep-seated
for privacy in the people of the Gulf. Whether a reflection
e teachings of Islam[14] or an outcome of a history of living

Interface between new
construction and an existing
heritage structure at Msheireb
Downtown Doha. A new
urban space is created in
between the buildings.

Sharjah Investment and
Development Authority

Heart of Sharjah

Sharjah, UAE

due for completion 2025

The inward-looking urban form
and the length of the *sikka* result
in a public realm that is activated
by elements that engage the
senses.

right: Courtyard in the Heart of
Sharjah. Internal courtyards are
intimately scaled and have explicit
historical references.

-sh desert conditions, this need for privacy is challenged
- constant contact and exposure encountered in
-geneous social settings. Israa Mahdi found that parks
-ther existing planned components of the public realm
-t fit the lifestyle and habits of some residents of Sharjah
-bourhoods.[15] This suggests that the kind of diversity and
- interaction envisioned for the public realm might be
-ul thinking. The planners for the Doha project speculate
-his 'social experiment'[16] might work for citizens who are
- professionals, but that remains an open question.
-t the same time, changes in social mores may also work
-st attempts to attract citizens back to the urban core.
-apid increase in wealth experienced by Gulf societies
-een accompanied by the evolution of more formal
-onships among households.[17] The easy camaraderie
-lent in neighbourhoods in the past has been supplanted
-ore formal, and more elaborate, forms of interaction.
-en who would call to each other from adjacent homes or
-ops now must invite each other and prepare extensively
-ese visits. The physical configuration of today's
-bourhoods means that travel, even to nearby homes,
- be by car. Women who have experienced the old and
-ew report that such meetings take so much effort that
-o-face interactions have declined, though that may not
- only reason. Is this kind of social change already deeply
-ined or can living in dense urban settings rekindle more
-l interactions? These observations may not hold for
- professionals.

-he Doha project also appears to take on an important
-n challenge that has largely been avoided in other real-
- development projects in the Gulf. That is, how can the
-ional, horizontally oriented neighbourhood be re-created
-ay's vertically oriented structures? The proposed use
- atrium in housing for citizens[18] presents interesting
-bilities, but it is not clear if this 'private *fereej*' is simply
-ourtyard house configured vertically rather than a
-bourhood. Khaled Galal Ahmed also speculates on the
-of creating neighbourhoods for UAE citizens in high-
-uildings and identifies the issues (social connectedness,
-ity, privacy), but he does not provide any paradigm-
-ng ideas for this '*fareej* in the sky'.[19]

der Consequences

-ew hearts for Doha and Sharjah 'fit' the body into which
-are being inserted in some respects. However, in terms
-ore profound psycho-social needs, these developments
- be less well suited. There is also little evidence to suggest
-hese projects have been considered in terms of impact
-e broader context. Dramatic interventions of this kind
-mplex urban systems can have unintended, unexpected
-mergent consequences.[20] What will happen to the people
-usinesses that are being displaced by these projects?
-they simply be scattered about and then absorbed
-other parts of the city, or will this displacement have
-ptive consequences in places to which people relocate?
-e are some of the fundamental challenges facing the
-ping attempts to re-create traditional urban form instead
-ore incremental and perhaps informal change that better
-orts with a complex reality. ⌂

Notes
1. Anne Coles and Peter Jackson, *Windtower*, Stacey International (London), 2007.
2. Herbert J Gans, 'The Human Implications of Current Redevelopment and Relocation Planning', *Journal of the American Institute of Planners*, 25 (1), 1959, pp 15–26.
3. Msheireb Downtown Doha Project Overview: http://mdd.msheireb.com/exploreproject/projectoverview.aspx.
4. http://shurooq.gov.ae/en/project/our-developments/heart-of-sharjah.html.
5. Rosanna Law and Kevin Underwood, 'Msheireb Heart of Doha: An Alternative Approach to Urbanism in the Gulf Region', *International Journal of Islamic Architecture*, 1 (1), 2012, pp 131–47.
6. Nadine Scharfenort, 'Large-Scale Urban Regeneration: A New "Heart" for Doha', Arabian Humanities, 2013: http://cy.revues.org/2532 (accessed 2 May 2014).
7. Design services have been or are being provided by Adjaye Associates, Allies and Morrison, Eric Parry Architects, Gensler, HOK, John McAslan & Partners, Mangera Yvars, Mossessian + Partners, and Squire and Partners. See www.msheireb.com/Portals/0/Documents/pdf/Fact%20Sheet%20-%20Eng-%20101013.pdf.
8. William Hanley, 'Exhibition Review: The 11th Sharjah Biennial', *Architectural Record*, 9 April 2013: http://archrecord.construction.com/news/2013/04/130409-Sharjah-Biennial-Review-OFFICE-SANAA-Ole-Scheeren-Studio-Mumbai.asp.
9. http://www.daralomran.com/arch/?portfolio=heart-of-sharjah&lang=en&pageid=162.
10. *Ibid*.
11. Coles and Jackson, op cit.
12. Law and Underwood, *op cit*, Figures 10a and 10b. Credits for these images are wrongly assigned in the book. The image credited to Mossessian & Partners is actually by Allies and Morrison, and vice versa. References in the above text are to the corrected credits.
13. Shaima Al Harmoudi, Morphological Evolution of Residential Neighborhoods: The Case of Sharjah', Unpublished final project, Master of Urban Planning Program, American University of Sharjah, 2010.
14. Mohsen Kadivar, 'An Introduction to the Public and Private Debate in Islam', *Social Research*, 70 (3), 2003, pp 559–680.
15. Israa Mahdi, 'Use of Public Areas in Emirati Residential Neighborhoods: Preliminary Findings from Sharjah, UAE', Unpublished final project, Master of Urban Planning Program, American University of Sharjah, 2013.
16. Law and Underwood, *op cit*, p 146.
17. Shaima Al Harmoudi and Varkki Pallathucheril, 'Household Relocation and the Restructuring of Social Relationships: Insights from Sharjah, UAE', paper presented at the 26th Annual Congress of the Association of European Schools of Planning, Ankara, Turkey July 2012.
18. Law and Underwood, *op cit*, Figure 15f.
19. Khaled Galal Ahmed, 'A "Fareej-in-the-Sky": Towards a Community-oriented Design for High-rise Residential Buildings in the UAE', *Open House International* 37 (1), 2012, pp 48–70.
20. Robert J Chaskin, Mark L Joseph, Sara Voelker and Amy Dworsky, 'Public Housing Transformation and Resident Relocation: Comparing Destinations and Household Characteristics in Chicago', *Cityscape* 14 (1), 2012, pp 183–214.

Todd Reisz

'1971 marked not only a beginning, but also an end of Dubai as those who knew it knew it.' Taking 1971 as a watershed moment for Dubai's development, architect, educator and author **Todd Reisz** examines how the acceptance and then refutation of the 1971 Plan for Dubai, drawn up by British architect John R Harris, proved pivotal.

Future Flyovers
Dubai in 1971

Making plans for cities is usually about establishing and ensuring stability. By th time Dubai's 1971 masterplan was issued however, the emirate city's leadership – namely Sheikh Rashid bin Saeed Al Makt – had decided that such a projection of stability was not sensible, even in the fac instability on all fronts. Assertive leaders British advice and some geopolitical happenstance had made manifest by the a fusion of a pre-modern and modern cit along the easily identifiable Dubai Creek. Triggered by the tapping of commercial amounts of oil in 1969, the 1971 plan was intended to address the growth predicted result from oil wealth, but it also came at inauspicious moment – or maybe that wa the point. 1971 marked not only a beginn but also an end of Dubai as those who kr it knew it.

In 1969, giant oil storage tanks (each larg than any building ever built in Dubai thus were launched 19 kilometres (12 miles) fr Dubai Creek and floated out to sea. Britis architect John R Harris, already a decade in consultative service to Sheikh Rashid, and the author of Dubai's first masterplan was commissioned to lay out how this ne wealth would translate into more tarmac concrete and steel.[1] By the time Harris delivered the plan, 21 months after the la of Dubai's oil industry, there was already end. The promise of oil was never realise commercial quantities were limited, and focus of the new plan shifted to 'maintair [Dubai's] pre-eminent position as a tradin centre' wherein oil wealth would not be necessary.[2]

Dubai in Question
In the 1960s, Dubai's leadership worked with its British counterparts to develop essential infrastructure and a basic munic bureaucracy. However, the following deca was really more about Abu Dhabi (thoug Dubai was still growing). One British trav writer, Jonathan Raban, noted that Abu Dhabi was the place of 'the temporary an the brand-new', whereas Dubai was like a 'well-worn tweed jacket. It didn't reek of paint.'[3] Raban published his account at th end of the 1970s, when Dubai was alread forging ahead with major expansion proj but his account provides the evidence that the city's heart was still at the Creek, when it seems Rashid was already focuse elsewhere.

The early part of the 1970s found Dubai becoming part of a new nation called the United Arab Emirates. Abu Dhabi, not Du was scheduled to be the capital. There se to be no available documents that explici reveal Sheikh Rashid's views about the implications the British withdrawal would

for Dubai's developing position in the
[...]. While anecdotes and off-the-record
[...]ments are unreliable, there may well
[...] been some concerns, especially in light
[...]ntemporary reports on the region in
[...]national newspapers: their focus was
[...]u Dhabi, the holder of the oil the world
[...]ed and now a new nation's capital. If
[...]Dhabi was the capital city, then what
[...] Dubai? Second city? A commercial
[...]sity? Even in the early pages of the
[...]planning document, Harris noted that
[...]nent nationhood 'will undoubtedly have
[...]derable effects on the planning and
[...]opment of Dubai'. Those effects were
[...]ecessarily positive.

1971 Plan:
cceptance and a Refutation

[...]he end of the 1970s Dubai seemed to a
[...]lling observer like a stable, established
[...]hen that was only in comparison to
[...]Dhabi. Life in Dubai was in constant
[...]ition. The city would begin the decade
[...] a population between 59,000 and
[...]00 (there was no official or dependable
[...]e), but at the end of the decade the
[...]lation was registered at three times
[...] of the larger estimate (according to
[...]ctions on which the plan is based, the
[...]lation was expected to grow to 200,000
[...]rlier than 1990). The 1971 plan noted that
[...]ajority of people still moved around
[...]ot, but the demand for roads already
[...]aced their construction.

John R Harris and Partners

Cover of the 'Dubai
Development Plan Review'

1971

The cover of the 1971 plan features an
aerial view from the Deira section of
Dubai overlooking Dubai Creek and
the Bur Dubai district. Port Rashid
can be seen in the background. The
city's future development would focus
beyond the bounds of this photograph.

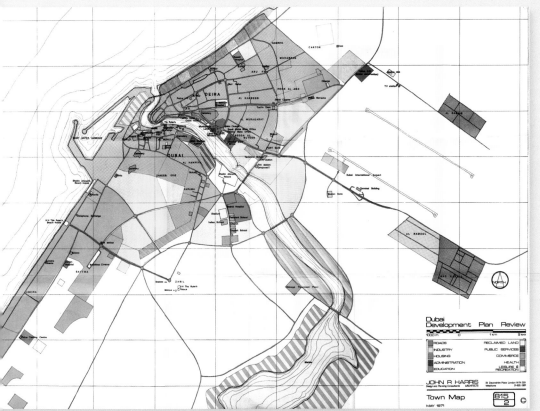

John R Harris
and Partners

Town Map

'Dubai Development
Plan Review'

1971

Plan with road network and
land-use designations that
was submitted with the
development review text. As
with the text, the map still
focuses attention on the city
around the creek. Roads that
continue beyond the map's
edges suggest Dubai's future
expansion.

101

The complex that would eventually be known as the World Trade Centre included a Hilton Hotel, a theatre, an exhibition centre and the 39-storey Sheikh Rashid Tower. Situated at Dubai's largest roundabout, it would direct the city's growth from Dubai Creek (top right) towards the Abu Dhabi road, later named Sheikh Zayed Road.

Harris tried to capture the momentum by referring to Dubai as a 'Capital City' in the plan, but that title would describe a different place in a matter of months. Dubai's bustling city core was not going to compete with Abu Dhabi's ascendancy. In the end, the masterplan addresses, but also falls victim to, this indeterminate, transformative moment. The complications led to an intrinsic conflict in the plan – one between responsible urbanism and geopolitical survival.

One might suspect this conflict resulted from the tension between the planner's professionalism and realpolitik. If the former is represented in Harris's moderate calls for appreciating Dubai's historical character and regulating how the new and necessary interacted with that character, then the latter was represented in the drawn plan, which revealed a city reaching for new territory.

Planning by Text

By the time the 1971 plan was being draf[t] Harris had already witnessed the deviatio[n] from the low-rise development called for [in] his 1960 plan. The city had wisely accepte[d] (probably because of financial constraint[s]) Harris's recommendation to preserve the[ir] existing fabric with gradual insertions of modern amenities. Further, the new stre[et] of Dubai adhered to the plan's proposed system of roads and principles that inclu[de] measures such as separation between ca[rs] and pedestrians. However, Harris was we[ll] aware of the car's looming domination o[f] city and the accommodating infrastructu[re] that would only fuel that domination (highways, bridges, tunnels, car park). N[o] needed, land at major intersections was [to be] reserved for the 'future flyovers' this imm[ense] traffic would require. Although there wa[s] traffic congestion at times at the Al Makto[um] Bridge, the single crossing of Dubai Cree[k] the plan found resistance to future conge[stion] build-up to be futile, even though it mad[e] mention of a bus service and an eventua[l] monorail system.

Harris dedicated a great deal of the docu[ment] to observations about preservation and conservation. He addressed the need for building regulations to protect Dubai's 'physical character'.[4] Nevertheless, the pl[an] accepted the reality of increased density [at] Dubai Creek and at Cinema Square (now [ ] Square or Baniyas Square) and the pendi[ng] development of the Deira Corniche where [a] 25-storey Hyatt hotel would open in a fe[w] years. In regard to the large-scale perspe[ctive] he insisted that growth still be focused o[n] the Creek, the city's historical and econor[mic] basis: 'Both from a functional and an aest[hetic] viewpoint, therefore, developing Dubai should still be centred on the Creek.'[5] The [ ] included, once again, his recommendatio[n to] build an identifiable civic centre on the C[reek]

Tanks

, UAE

derwater storage tanks
y the Chicago Bridge
any were among the
rge-scale infrastructure
ts intended to contribute
transformation of Dubai's
my. They were launched
with a public ceremony at
s now the site of Madinat
rah. In the end, Dubai's
re oil supply proved
i, and its focus on
mic growth had to return
i.

While the document acknowledged that the city needed to grow, it maintained the assumption that the Creek should remain the centre of that growth, resulting in either increased density in some areas or continuing development eastward. Areas for expansion included the coastal zone 'up-Creek' further inland, a site designated for 'high-quality housing' and a marina. This assumed direction of growth would continue to guide planners engaged by the municipality despite the increasing evidence that the city was moving southward, along the Gulf, with or without a plan. This conflict between what the plan represented and what happened is further accentuated by the fact that Harris's plan makes only one mention of the 'Abu Dhabi road', which would eventually come to be known as Sheikh Zayed Road, the spine of development for Dubai's expansion in the direction of Abu Dhabi.

Plan as Image

The plan as represented in the drawing remained conceptual, representing broad-stroke land-use designations and the suggestion of an expanded road network. The Abu Dhabi road, rendered as a tenuous line, is by no means the widest road featured on the plan. Thicker lines were reserved for the ring roads serving both sides of the Creek. Although the plan's text held onto the idea that the Creek would remain the centre of the city, the drawn plan allowed another tendency, and one that characterised Dubai's eventual pattern of growth. The edges suggest the plan moves beyond the paper; the thin orange lines moving beyond the edges of the page, rather than the swaths of land-use colours, would prove the most prophetic. The current-day observer cannot help but see the city stretching to the south (left), along Jumeirah Road and the Abu Dhabi road, much of which remains undesignated (white) in the plan, but development in the 1970s would reveal that this was where and how the city grew. Dubai's developers would embrace Harris's call for low density where it was needed to spread the city's reach further. Harris's plan paints this area blue, as solely residential, and this was maintained in the low-rise villas in Jumeirah. The white along the Abu Dhabi road would eventually form a stretched, frenzied spine to replace the Creek as the city's defining element. But in 1971, that future focus was still blank on Dubai's plan.

View from the Sheikh
Rashid Tower looking
over the Dubai–Abu
Dhabi Road in the
direction of Abu Dhabi
to the south

Dubai, UAE

c 1978

The road would later become
known as Sheikh Zayed Road.
Along with a scattering of
other high-rise buildings, the
15-storey World Trade Centre
Apartments, part of the Word
Trade Centre axis, were open
and offering 'luxury furnished'
accommodation.

At the time the plan was issued, the
modernisation of the Creek's harbour facilities
was still being refined with more dredging,
and nearby Port Rashid was not even
finished. Harris's document made it clear
that there was more to achieve in this area.
Ultimately, however, the plan's hopes and
expectations for the city around the Creek
were less important than its suggestions of
expansion. By the time Sheikh Rashid held
his commissioned plan in his hands, his
ambitions had departed from Harris's textual
prescription and followed instead the orange
lines beyond the page.

Why would Dubai's leadership deem it
necessary to prefer sprawl to density? The
are at least two suspected reasons: the fir
related to Dubai's domestic politics; and t
second was a response to the city's new
status within a nation. As Harris noted in
document, land for new development aro
the Creek was difficult to obtain. Sheikh
Rashid could not afford to buy out proper
owners; there had been some deals, som
trades, but land holders could benefit mo
by becoming entrepreneurs themselves.
Some of Deira's unnavigable streets are
a result of the limits of state authority.
Therefore, Sheikh Rashid had to focus wh
land was not so easily claimed by others.
The second reason for preferring sprawl
to density was perhaps due to the need
to express the limits of Dubai's existence.
Sheikh Rashid did not necessarily envisio
that Dubai would fully develop from its
border with Sharjah to that with Abu Dha
but quickly occupying the borders physica
expressed the limits contained within
diplomatic agreements.

Let the 1970s Begin

Sheikh Rashid's expansionary determination is reflected in the city's mythology. The story goes that he rang Neville Allen, an engineer and resident consultant to the ruler, very early one morning and asked to meet him at Dubai's southernmost outpost, Jebel Ali. Sheikh Rashid is said to have told Allen he wanted to build a port there. Allen is said then to have given an immediate but rough cost estimate.[7] Some 30 kilometres (19 miles) beyond the bounds of the 1971 masterplan, Port Jebel Ali would not officially be announced until 1976, but its beginnings occur within a matter of months after the 1971 plan was issued.

The story is wrapped in a legend of tabula rasa, of a leader looking out at a blank canvas of desert and seeing a future. But the site was hardly blank. Somewhere near where Sheikh Rashid rendezvoused with Allen stood a radio tower that had been built on the site to establish communications with the rest of the world. When Sheikh Rashid had designated the site for the tower, the land was still a contested border with Abu Dhabi.[8] Whereas the radio tower built in the 1960s asserted his territorial claim, the world's largest port definitively established the physical limits of Dubai in light of its subjugation to a larger national project. The legend of tabula rasa quickly fades to a story of land known for its real-estate value, if not just in geopolitical terms. Sheikh Rashid's scheme for a port, and potentially more, right at the border of Abu Dhabi, expressed the broad sweep of coastal expansion that Dubai could provide for development, a strategy that dealt with the reality that it would be pre-oil successes in business and trade that would allow the city to continue to survive among the forces beyond its borders.

After submitting to the municipality a plan without a Port Jebel Ali, John Harris received another commission from Sheikh Rashid: an 'international exhibition centre' that would later become known as the World Trade Centre, with the most conspicuous element being Sheikh Rashid Tower, a 39-storey tower that was set to reign as the Middle East's tallest skyscraper into the 1990s. Perhaps the complex was Sheikh Rashid's negotiation with Harris's consistent counsel to develop a civic centre along the Creek. Civic would be found somewhere among hospitality, trade and exhibition. Instead of centring the city, the project would be the pivotal point for the city's growth along the road to Port Jebel Ali and Abu Dhabi, a highway of skyscrapers the world would not soon forget. ∆

Notes

1. John Harris was an indubitable presence in Sheikh Rashid's management of his city. Sheikh Rashid first met Harris when he arrived in Dubai as a prospective candidate to draw the city's first town plan in 1959. Upon agreeing to do this job, Harris also took on the commission to design the coast's first hospital into something more than a concrete-block shed. Harris had maintained a recurring and stable presence in Sheikh Rashid's ring of advisers and was a close consultant, if not mentor, to Dubai's fledgling planning department. This led to Harris's engagement to draw up Dubai's 1971 plan. The author thanks Jill Harris and Mark Harris for their continuing help and advice for this article.
2. John R Harris Architects and Planning Consultants, 'Dubai Development Plan Review', May 1971. For a published version of this document's texts, see John Harris, 'Dubai Development Plan Review, 1971', in *Development Plans of the GCC States*, 1962–1995, Archive Editions (Slough, UK), 1994.
3. Jonathan Raban, *Arabia: Through the Looking Glass*, Picador (London), reprint, 1987, p 164.
4. Harris had co-written, with the Dubai Municipality, a building regulations code, which was instituted in 1969.
5. John R Harris Architects and Planning Consultants, *op cit*.
6. Frauke Heard-Bey, *From Trucial States to United Arab Emirates*, Motivate Publishing (Dubai), 2004.
7. Graeme Wilson, *Rashid's Legacy: The Genesis of the Maktoum Family and the History of Dubai*, Media Prima (Dubai), reprint, 2006, p 368.
8. Stephen J Ramos, *Dubai Amplified: The Engineering of a Port Geography*, Ashgate (London), p 107.

al view of a
dential villa
opment

, UAE

73

ng, developed along the
rimarily at first for Western
iates, characterised the
ow-density development
e 1971 plan's expanded
y encouraged.

Foster + Partners

Masdar Institute

Masdar City

Abu Dhabi, UAE

2010

Sustainability in the desert. Masdar Institute stands out from its sandy surroundings and from other urban developments in Abu Dhabi.

Urban a Architec Sustaina in the Gu

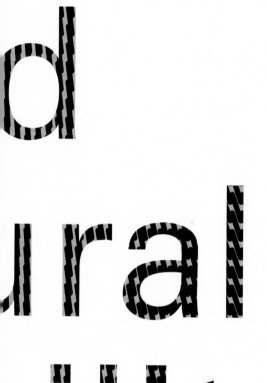

Interior courtyard of the Masdar Institute with wall openings of various sizes.

Robert Cooke

What is the impact of rapid urbanisation on sustainable development, such as that experienced by cities in the Gulf? **Robert Cooke**, an Associate Sustainability Consultant at Buro Happold, based in Dubai, seeks to answer this question. He asks what the real contribution might be of the implementation of recent sustainable policies and urban projects, and what more needs to be done to improve the Gulf's ecological footprint and the water–energy nexus.

The term 'sustainable development' is commonly defined by the summary quotation from *Our Common Future* (Bruntland Report) published by the World Commission on Environment and Development in 1987:

> Development that meets the needs of the present without compromising the ability of future generations to meet their ow needs.[1]

The need to ensure sustainable development is widely agreed upo However, since 1987 most countries and regions around the world have largely failed to implement comprehensive sustainability measures, and in most cases the situation is significantly worse than 27 years ago. Humanity's ecological footprint exceeded the earth's biocapacity by more than 50 per cent in 2008 from near par in 1987.[2]

Over this period the economy of the UAE has risen by a factor of 10 in current US dollars terms. As shown in the table here, other countries within the Gulf Cooperation Council (GCC) region have experienced similar economic growth.

The increases in economic activity have resulted in corresponding increases in the construction of buildings and cities. Indeed, cities such as Dubai and Doha are now barely recognisable This article discusses the impact of rapid development on cities in t Gulf.

Impacts on the Natural Environment

The Living Planet Index Ecological Footprint has been used consistently for the measurement of ecological footprints for a sustained period. It provides a useful assessment method for understanding relative impacts, tracking change, reviewing trends and for target setting. Using this tool, the current (published) ecological footprint of Gulf countries are estimated to be as follows Kuwait: 9.72 global hectares per capita; Qatar: 11.68 global hectares per capita; Saudi Arabia: 3.99 global hectares per capita; UAE: 8.44 global hectares per capita.[3] When considered in relation to a global average biocapacity of 1.8 global hectares per person (and a much lower regional biocapacity), there is clearly overconsumption and a reliance on imports of resources.

The ecological footprint of Arab countries has changed significantly in the past 50 years, from a position of having a biocapacity surplus prior to 1978, to one of significant deficit now with consumption exceeding capacity in 2005 by a ratio of 2 to 1, and biocapacity rapidly falling.[4] Approximately two-thirds of the ecological footprint of Gulf countries is carbon emissions, which have been the main growth factor since records began. The remaining emissions largely relate to the interrelation between food production, fishing and consumption, stemming from the use of artificial fertilisers, a scarcity of groundwater increasing reliance on desalinated water, and the use of fossil fuels for each step in the production and supply chain. The relationships are also linked further due to the need for water for fossil fuel extraction and heat rejection. Although the footprint of food production is relatively low the environmental costs of food imports are not accounted for and remain partly 'hidden' within the carbon account.

Also important is the presence of the water–energy nexus across the region. Awareness of the nexus is growing globally, but is particularly poignant for this region where local economies are relia on the presence of low-cost fuel and water, and on the trade exchang of fuel exports and food imports to support expanding cities. In Sau Arabia it is estimated that up to 9 per cent of the total annual electrical energy consumption may be attributed to groundwater pumping and desalination. In the UAE this figure is closer to 20 per cent of total electricity consumption for desalination, and these figures are rising as new desalination capacity is developed.[5]

GDP growth for Gulf Countries

1987 to 2012

Source: *World Bank, World Databank, World Development Indicators,* The World Bank Group (Washington DC): http:// databank.worldbank.org/data/home.aspx

COUNTRY	1987 GDP*	2012 GDP*
Bahrain	$3 bn	$30 bn
Kuwait	$22 bn	$183 bn
Qatar	$5 bn	$192 bn
Saudi Arabia	$86 bn	$711 bn
UAE	$36 bn	$384 bn

*current US$

er + Partners
───────────────
ar Institute Laboratories
───────────────
ar City

Dhabi, UAE
───────────────

ic vehicles (EVs) are running on
geable batteries using power
Masdar City's photovoltaic solar
The unique technology behind the
as been adapted to suit the UAE's
e climatic conditions.

Policy Responses

Organisations such as the Masdar Institute, the King Abdullah University of Science and Technology (KAUST) and the Qatar Foundation have taken steps to improve research, development and deployment of renewable and efficient technologies in the region, such as solar desalination, solar farms and saltwater greenhouses. However, implementation of new technology will be gradual and heavily dependent on long-term investment. There have also been movements to raise awareness and to implement rating systems and green regulations in the UAE and Qatar over the past five years. The Estidama Pearl Rating System became mandatory in Abu Dhabi (2010), in 2012 Sheikh Mohammed bin Rashid Al Maktoum announced the implementation of the UAE Green Economy which led to the inauguration of the Dubai Supreme Council of Energy (DSCE), which then subsequently published the Dubai Integrated Energy Strategy for 2030 and the Dubai State of Energy Report. These reports present a target to reduce energy demand by 30 per cent by 2030 and outline plans for a wide range of energy-efficient programmes to reduce energy consumption in existing facilities and infrastructure. Numerous measures are now coming into force to support these energy-reduction targets, including the Dubai Green Building Regulations (DGBR) for new buildings and the implementation of the UAE Energy Efficiency Lighting Standard.

It is notable that in addition to mandatory local codes such as Estidama and the DGBR, the UAE was also recently included in a table of the top 10 Green Building Nations for the number of LEED-certified projects in the country, which now total more than 1.8 million square metres (19.3 million square feet).

Saudi Arabia has recently introduced the KSA insulation law,[6] and plans to construct the carbon-neutral King Abdullah City for Atomic and Renewable Energy (K.A.CARE), which will incorporate bespoke green building regulations. The King Abdullah Financial District is a major development currently under construction, committed to obtaining LEED certification and hence setting a major precedent for the country.

Skyline
───────────────
Dubai, UAE
───────────────
2014

The rapid growth of Dubai has led to an ever-changing skyline, but very few of these buildings or their environs have been designed with sustainability in mind. The evening smog provides a subtle hue to this image, but symbolises a reliance on road transport.

Bahrain recently completed the first LEED-certified buildings in the country and has announced that strategic affordable housing schemes will be accredited using LEED or equivalent green rating systems.

Qatar has recently implemented the Global Sustainability Assessment System (GSAS); though a voluntary system, it is employed by many private and government development companies. At a strategic level, the state is carrying out studies to reduce energy and water demands. Though as yet there are few completed building examples, the LEED rating system will be incorporated in major developments in progress, including the Doha Metro, the Msheireb Downtown Doha project (masterplanned by Allies and Morrison) and the National Museum of Qatar (Ateliers Jean Nouvel). Notably, Msheireb is expected to become the world's largest community of LEED-certified buildings, and is based on core environmental design principles.

Urban Design Projects

These policy developments have led to changes in practice and improvements in stakeholder awareness, resulting in a number of exemplar projects across the region (both newbuild and refurbishments).

Foster + Partners' ambitious 2008 masterplan for Masdar City was based on some very grand notions that were perhaps beyond the technical, supplier and economic capacity of the region. Some of its main features were zero carbon, self-generation, no cars, highly shaded external areas and efficient buildings. The original plan was to meet a large number of targets that have now been refined to a more grounded 10 core key performance indicators. Though not fully delivered as originally devised, Masdar has been influential across the region and beyond in terms of its energy technology development through the application and testing of innovative solutions, the Future Build portal for sustainable materials, awareness raising of building-integrated photovoltaics (BIPV) versus ground-based photovoltaics, application of different materials and so on. With more realistic aims, Masdar City is now being developed at a rapid pace, hosting world-leading projects and with exceptional environmental performance.

One reflection from the Masdar project is how to ensure economic, social and environmental sustainability for such a large and ambitious project from the initial phase through to completion. In a region with such rapid growth and changing perspectives, how can a development be seeded to grow organically yet in a structured and compliant manner? Is it possible to balance the cost of initial infrastructure, flexibility to adapt to changing market conditions, and the need to create social attraction and critical mass?

Msheireb Downtown Doha (see pp 42–9 of this issue) is being constructed on a 31-hectare (77-acre) site in central Doha, largely within one super-phase due to the inner-city nature, and hence overcoming phasing and critical mass issues. This high-density, mixed-use development aims to create a city heart integrated with the metro and also incorporating a heritage element, with shaded external environments and high energy and water efficiency based on passive design principles.

Another important project is the King Abdullah City for Atomic and Renewable Energy, a sustainable city planned for the outskirts of Riyadh. As with Masdar, K.A.CARE is a new city concept on the fringes of an existing conurbation. It will generate all of its own energy and will set a unique precedent in Saudi Arabia. At this point, very little is published relating to the project, but it will be interesting to see how it develops in comparison with Masdar and Msheireb.

With the changes in policy highlighted above, these commitments to exemplary sustainable urban designs will hopefully be followed by many more, and recent research seems to suggest that the shifts in strategy are having the desired impact. In its study of *World Green Building Trends* in 2013, McGraw Hill Construction summarised the following for the UAE:

> the UAE sample firms are overwhelmingly planning green in new green institutional projects, indicating heavy influence of the government on the market today – and in the future. Education will be important across stakeholder groups.[7]

It also noted that the 'green share' of project activity of the UAE respondents interviewed was 51 per cent, third only, from the sample countries, to Singapore (66 per cent) and the UK (52 per cent). The number of highly green-involved UAE firms in 2012 was nearly five times higher than in 2009. The top triggers for building green were: regulations (55 per cent), client demand (50 per cent) and market demand (32 per cent). The top barriers were: higher first cost (82 per cent) followed by lack of public awareness (50 per cent) and lack of market demand (42 per cent).

Dubai Metro

Dubai, UAE

2014

The Dubai Metro is very popular and is supported by a feeder bus network. The two original lines are being extended and added to, with up to six lines planned in total and a new tram system, creating an integrated network in the high-density Marina and Al Sufouh districts.

Architects

Ling Towers

i, UAE

for completion

perspective of Sterling
rs 1 and 2.

developed by Omniyat
Business Bay district
bai, Sterling Towers 1
are a great example of
ve environmental design
gh the use of optimised
tation, glazing distribution
external shading.

ds Bagot

lege of the North Atlantic

a, Qatar

5

occupancy evaluation of the external
es has shown how careful design can
ficantly increase external comfort.

The college is a
good example of
practical sustainable
design in Qatar,
providing strong solar
protection internally
and externally to
deliver comfortable
environments.

SOM

Sheikh Khalifa Medical City

Abu Dhabi, UAE

due for completion 2018

Sheikh Khalifa Medical City, winner of numerous awards, will be a 750-bed medical complex in the heart of Abu Dhabi. Envisioned as a 'city within a city', the design endeavours to defy the typical model of a medical centre and create a bustling campus-like environment of distinct character, with vibrant public spaces and a sense of community.

However, such is the extent of the problem that the rate of change is still not sufficient to overcome the current ecological footprint disparity, and sustainable approaches are still not prevalent (especially outside of Abu Dhabi). Ultimately, increased awareness and the role of society are crucial for long-lasting effective change. The realisation that 'buildings don't use energy: people do'[8] shows that making a real difference in delivering sustainable buildings requires encouraging and enabling users to reduce consumption, and not just applying technological fixes. Abu Dhabi is a leading light in the region for implementing change through the introduction of its Estidama programme, but developing and delivering this ground-breaking system was not without its own challenges. From the outside it is easy to see Estidama as an overwhelming success, but not all stakeholders were supportive initially, perhaps partially because of the speed of implementation thrust upon them.

Some of the lessons learnt from the Estidama experience are that throughout the development and implementation of an environmental rating system or regulation, process-specific consideration has to be given to issues such as: relevance to the cultural and natural context; the difficulty level of achieving credits and understanding requirements for compliance; cost implications (process, construction and operational); alignment with government policies; availability of skill sets in the market; and materials and products supply chain readiness. This takes time, care and significant sustained effort, and each of the countries across the GCC now needs to implement similar moves.

General Hospital Approach perspective of Sheikh Khalifa Medical City. Informed by historical regional precedents and designed for environmental performance, the hospital is notable for its strong facade treatment that significantly reduces solar loads yet allows daylight and views for its occupants, which helped to achieve a 2 Pearl Estidama rating at the design stage.

Pediatric Hospital Approach perspective of Sheikh Khalifa Medical City showing strong massing, shallow forms and heavy facade solar shading.

ssive resource consumption in the Gulf is critical. It will impact
conomies, societies and policies in the region. All urban and
ing designs therefore need to be adapted to a new reality, and
ing buildings refurbished.

New developments in the Gulf largely still ignore sustainability,
many projects still below the necessary requirements for
ation due to a lack of sufficient thought, detail and application
e design and construction stage. Though not published,
are numerous stories of new and high-profile buildings that
ear impossible to maintain, have leaky facades (leading to
o and mould), include oversized and under-commissioned
ms, provide inadequate internal environments and are more
iability than an asset to their owners. With a predominance
velopers looking to quickly sell properties off-plan, without
g policy incentives this trend is likely to continue.

On some projects, not enough time is being spent designing
supervising construction. However, there is now a visible
tion in the attitudes of contractors across the region, with
more attention to environmental controls, building quality
providing proof that the building meets design requirements
to handover. This is especially the case in Abu Dhabi due to
mandatory introduction of the Estidama Pearl Rating System,
h at its most basic level is a quality-control check that is
ence-based and monitored closely throughout construction.
lso due to the success of Estidama, other regions and
tries now have evidence on their doorstep that significant and
change is possible. Notably in Dubai, developers are realising
they have a problematic legacy from buildings delivered in
revious boom. There is also a recognisable 'value' premium
igh-quality and sustainably located properties with access to
o stations and a sense of community.

New buildings are relatively easy to legislate for compared to
upgrading existing building stock. The sustainability knowledge
'capacity' for new construction in the Gulf still feels around 10
years behind more advanced countries like the UK and Germany,
and the industry is just coming to terms with what is required
for designing sustainable new buildings as standard practice
rather than as a special measure. Meanwhile, the more advanced
nations are now struggling to understand how to close the
'design gap' between projected design performance and actual
building performance, and how to address the existing building
stock, which is where the largest sustainability gains exist. A large
proportion of existing buildings in the Gulf are leaky, insufficiently
insulated, heavily glazed and poorly maintained, and in general
not designed for the longer term. This is an issue that leads to high
resource consumption levels, but is not currently being addressed.
Therefore, despite recent progress in new building design
measures, there is still a long way to go in creating sustainable
cities in the region.

Thus it is important for policies to focus on the majority rather
than the minority. The first challenge is to ensure buildings are at
least fit for purpose and maintainable. The second challenge is to
address the need for education and awareness across all industry
stakeholders, to create sustainable and engaged communities.

Finally, there is still a significant lack of data and social
engagement in the process of design, construction and operation.
Every project will not be perfect, but we need evidence of the
performance (and lifecycle cost) of buildings and systems to help
recognise best practice and learn from experience. This will allow
those in the field to experiment with more confidence and establish
tried and tested measures that improve the wider industry. The
region is still at the beginning of the curve and the rate of change
needs to increase. Sharing of best practice and proof of value-
benefits will be essential for success. ᴆ

Notes
1. World Commission on Environment and
Development, *Our Common Future*, Oxford
University Press (Oxford), 1987, p 27.
2. WWF, *Living Planet Report 2012*, WWF International
(Gland, Switzerland), 2012: http://wwf.panda.org/
about_our_earth/all_publications/living_planet_
report/2012_lpr/.
3. *Ibid.*
4. Najim Saab (ed), *Arab Environment 5: Survival
Options – Ecological Footprint of Arab Countries*,
Arab Forum for Environment and Development
(Beirut), 2012: www.footprintnetwork.org/images/
article_uploads/Survival_Options_Eng.pdf.
5. Afreen Siddiqi and Laura Diaz Anadon, 'The
Water–Energy Nexus in Middle East and North Africa',
Energy Policy, 39(6), 2011, pp 4529-40.
6. Utilities Middle East, 'Thermal Insulation to be
Mandatory in Saudi Arabia', 26 March 2014: www.
utilities-me.com/article-2771-thermal-insulation-to-be-
mandatory-in-saudi-arabia/.
7. McGraw Hill Construction SmartMarket Report,
*World Green Building Trends: Business Benefits
Driving New and Retrofit Market Opportunities
in Over 60 Countries*, McGraw Hill Construction
(Bedford, MA), 2013, p 8: http://analyticsstore.
construction.com/index.php/world-green-building-
trends-smartmarket-report-2013.html.
8. Kathryn B Janda, 'Buildings Don't Use Energy:
People Do', PLEA2009 – 26th Conference on Passive
and Low Energy Architecture, Quebec City, Canada,
22–4 June 2009: www.eci.ox.ac.uk/publications/
downloads/janda09buildingsdont.pdf.

mal imaging camera results
_____

e thermal imaging tests can easily
int excessive air infiltration and thermal
ng which may be causing excessive
y use and uncontrolled moisture ingress.
varm conditions are perfect for mould
h, a major concern for indoor air quality
Gulf region.

Air pressure testing combined
with smoke and thermal imaging
_____

2012

These advanced envelope testing and
diagnostics methods are now being applied
regularly on new projects and increasingly for
existing buildings in the Gulf. With such high
external temperatures and humidity levels,
airtightness is a critical factor for healthy,
comfortable and efficient environments.

Jeffrey Willis

10 Years of Sustainable Initiatives in the Gulf Region

Fast Forwards

Over the last decade, sustainable initiatives have proliferated in the UAE through a disparate range of public and private sector efforts. **Jeffrey Willis**, Sustainability Leader for Arup in the Gulf, provides a comprehensive review of these enterprises, highlighting how momentum has been clustered in three distinct periods of activity: previous to 2006; 2006 to 2008; and then since the global financial crisis in 2008.

A major change has taken place in the construction industry in the Gulf region within the last 10 years. The speed of cha[nge] and the rate at which the Gulf has caught up with regions that were more advanced is unprecedented. This article looks at tha[t] change process as it has occurred, with a specific focus on sustainability. Although it concentrates on information from the UAE, similar activities have also taken pla[ce] elsewhere in the Gulf, and in the Middle E[ast] and North Africa (MENA) region, some of which are also referred to below.

A review of sustainability initiatives o[f] the last decade reveals an interesting mix[of] private-sector, public-sector and individua[l] small groups of individuals) efforts that h[ave] culminated in a significant change in the region. This relates not only to awareness[but] also to the implementation of the princip[les] of sustainability. The progress can rough[ly] be divided into three stages: pre-2006, wh[ich] was almost devoid of evidence of any acti[vity;] the period from 2006 to 2008, which mark[ed] an increase in awareness and the plantin[g of] the seeds of change; and implementation [and] achievement during 2008 to 2014.

Pre-2006

One significant piece of legislation before 2006 was the issue by the Dubai Municipa[lity] of Administrative Resolution 66 in 2003. T[his] was an advanced piece of work for its tim[e in] this part of the world. Not only did it set h[igh] standards for insulation and building fabr[ic] performance at a level about 7 per cent be[tter] than ASHRAE 90.1 (the US Green Council['s] Leadership in Energy & Environmental Design (LEED) benchmark), it also touche[d] on limiting glazed areas, using planting to provide shading, selecting orientation to b[est] advantage and controlling building envel[ope] air leakage and infiltration. It is unfortuna[te] that the implementation and policing of th[is] decree was difficult to achieve, apparently because the explosion in construction wa[s] too much for the authority to deal with, and many buildings constructed after 200[?] ignored in large part the intent of this far-sighted document.

Before 2006, individuals explored way[s] to promote and champion sustainable building design and construction. The mo[st] common outcome from these groups wa[s the] formation of Green Building Councils, wh[ich] sprang up in the UAE, Jordan, Qatar, Sau[di] Arabia, Egypt, Oman, Morocco, Kuwait an[d] Syria. In the years following their formatio[n] these bodies fulfilled important awarenes[s,] education and lobbying functions that we[re] essential to the developments that follow[ed]

2006–8

The Emirates Green Building Council was launched in June 2006, and became the eighth member of the World Green Building Council in September 2006.

A number of other milestones were reached in 2006. The Pacific Controls headquarters in Jebel Ali, Dubai, secured a LEED platinum certification, and a LEED Gold certification was attained by the Wafi City District Cooling Plant Building designed by architects Arif & Bintoak and engineers Green Technologies FZCO, both buildings being significantly more sustainable than the norm at that time, demonstrating extreme forward thinking on the part of the companies responsible for their development.

Also in 2006, Masdar (the company, not the city) was launched by the Abu Dhabi leadership with a mandate to advance renewable energy through education, research and development, investment and commercialisation, and a programme of research was begun that provided important data not previously available for the region. Masdar City has been an important location for the testing of theories and initiatives and has set very high benchmarks for its own development.

TECOM Investments, a member of Dubai Holding, is a global company dedicated to the development of knowledge industries and business growth. TECOM adopted a Sustainable Development Policy in 2006 with the aim of implementing LEED Certification and Green Building standards, promoting awareness campaigns and implementing initiatives in green procurement and recycling policies.

These activities, combined with the output from the Green Building Councils, led to increased recognition of the advantages of measuring sustainable design through assessment systems such as LEED, and the development of local assessment systems such as the Golden Pyramid in Egypt, the Qatar Sustainability Assessment System (QSAS) and the Estidama Pearl system in Abu Dhabi.

The Abu Dhabi Urban Planning Council (UPC) was created in 2007 and is the agency responsible for the future of Abu Dhabi's urban environments, and the expert authority behind the Abu Dhabi 2030 Urban Structure Framework Plan published in September 2007. Within the UPC, the Estidama department created the Pearl building assessment system and brought it into effect in April 2010. The requirements imposed by the UPC to instigate an Integrated Development Process, and the linking of that to the building permit process, was a demonstration of an understanding of the fundamental issues related to sustainable (good practice) building design and the need to impose a change for the better in the way of working in the building industry.

The baseline for any assessment system is marked by codes and standards. The Abu Dhabi Department of Municipal Affairs instigated the implementation of International Building Codes, which underpin the strong move towards better-quality buildings.

In Jebel Ali Free Zone, the regulatory authority, Trakhees-EHS, incorporated a number of credits from the LEED for New Construction rating system into its regulations with effect from January 2008, effectively setting a standard at LEED Silver. This was in direct response to a decree by Sheikh Mohammed bin Rashid Al Maktoum in November of 2007 to the effect that all new buildings in Dubai, as of the beginning of 2008, should be green buildings. The decree was also the trigger for the development of the Dubai Municipality Green Building Code that became mandatory in March 2014.

In Sharjah, UAE, the Ruler's Office and Directorate of Public Works issued Sustainable Development Guidelines in July 2008.

2008–14

Qatar's QSAS became active in 2010, and is now known by the name Global Sustainability Assessment System (GSAS). This momentum of activity, both by government departments and by the private sector, has resulted in some significant changes to the expectations of the market, and in the supply chain in response to these. It is therefore no surprise that the UAE's winning bid for the World Expo 2020 has 'sustainability' as one of the three sub-themes to the main theme of 'Connecting Minds, Creating the Future'; understanding of what is required to achieve such levels of sustainability will generate an international benchmark for others to emulate.

Challenges and Successes

An objection that was often raised to the move to more sustainable buildings was the observation that the required materials were not readily available and affordable in the Gulf markets. It is true that in 2006 it was difficult to find a low volatile organic compound (VOC) paint or a double-flush toilet in the Gulf for a reasonable price, and it is also true that as regulations have become mandatory, prices did rise temporarily as the market took advantage of a level of scarcity and a lack of knowledge to increase profits. More competition and better understanding have now matured the market with significant impact on materials availability and prices, such that it is no longer the case that these materials are difficult to find or necessarily more expensive.

However, construction budget and programme do remain an issue. The concern regarding sustainable construction in the UAE and Gulf Cooperation Council (GCC) markets is the lack of a robust sustainable supply chain. The building materials required to promote and enhance sustainability are likely to be imported, and this increases costs over locally produced cheaper, but less sustainable, products. It is also less sustainable to bring products greater distances, and it may take longer, impacting on programme. Contractors may be inclined to use more sustainable or environmentally friendly building elements for projects, but if their budget and programme do not afford them this leeway, then there will be some difficulties to address.

Contractors also face challenges responding to the requirements to reuse and recycle. Facilities to recycle waste have improved considerably within the last 10 years, but this is one area where there is room for significantly more provision.

What has been interesting to see developing are changes in attitudes towards socially related issues. An element of change that goes hand in hand with the move towards more sustainable building has been the impact on areas surrounding buildings, the perception of those surroundings and the infrastructure that serves the building, resulting in a major shift in attitudes towards the use of outside spaces.

From a situation at the beginning of the 21st century where the use of outside space between buildings was extremely limited, when it was assumed that occupied spaces within the built environment needed to be inside buildings and air conditioned, we have moved to the more general acceptance that properly designed outside spaces between buildings can be useful and enjoyable. In addition, properly designed shading and planting will enable much extended use of the outside space further into the summer months. This realisation has dramatically improved the design and layout of neighbourhoods, providing places where social gatherings can thrive and, for example, enabling the implementation of cycle- and walking paths in areas where they would not have existed previously.

Similarly, the attitude towards the provision of facilities to improve alternative transport solutions that reduce the number of cars has also experienced dramatic change. The acceptance that the quality of buses and

Reiser + Umemoto, RUR Architecture

O-14 Tower

Dubai

UAE

2011

The floor plan for the O-14 Tower shows the relationship between the glass curtain wall and the concrete exoskeleton, which functions as a shading device.

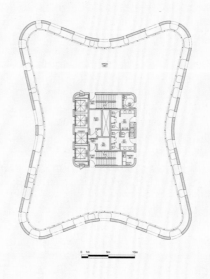

The irregular openings in the outer concrete exoskeleton provide passive protection from solar radiation and create a distinctive facade. The iconic appearance of the building results from a climate response rather than from the use of decorative elements.

ed by *mashrabiya*, the facade
e Abu Dhabi Investment
cil Headquarters was
ped to minimise the impact
nate. Supported by an
endent frame, panels coated
breglass open and close
ponse to the movement of
n.

bus-route provision needed to be improved such that all would be happy to travel on them; the provision of the Metro in Dubai and trams or monorails; the provision of decent water transportation; and the linking of bus services to all, represent a series of major steps forward in reducing the number of cars on the road.

Designs for New Buildings

The pursuit of sustainability and the regulations enforcing it have reasserted the need to design for function in buildings. The integrated design process enables the achievement of a more efficient building, and following the dictates of any of the assessment methods will ensure that commissioning takes place that allows a better chance that the buildings will be operated efficiently.

The requirements for buildings to be more sustainable have engendered various architectural conflicts, some of which should not perhaps have existed at all. A major conflict arises between the desire to produce buildings with large areas of vision glazing and the fact that this is a totally inappropriate solution for the Middle East climate and is clearly discouraged in all of the standards, guidelines and assessment systems that are in current use. This has led to some interesting responses in the design of building facades, examples of which are the Al Bahr Towers in Abu Dhabi by Aedas and Arup (2012) and Reiser + Umemoto's O-14 tower in Dubai (2011), where an external shading solution is provided to offset the impact of large areas of glazing.
January 2014 saw the completion of the King Fahad National Library Refurbishment and Extension. One of the most important cultural buildings in Saudi Arabia, the solution combines the challenge of designing within the existing building stock with respect for Arabian culture, and also makes extensive use of external shading.

The correct process is now being realised, which is to limit vision glazing to around 35 per cent of the facade related to the inside room face. This conclusion has been arrived at by a number of different agencies, and is the optimum for achieving a balance between the best use of natural daylight and the heat gain energy demand. An excellent example of this is the Siemens headquarters in Masdar City, Abu Dhabi (2013) by architects Sheppard Robson, which is the one place where the approach and intent seem to be 100 per cent correct.

Buildings have suffered from the extensive use of the word 'iconic' to describe the ultimate goal. The aspiration of achieving buildings that are described as 'best-in-class' and 'socially responsible' would be much more appropriate. Adopting a word that means 'symbol' or 'emblem' and evokes images of trophies to describe a building has resulted in the form being far more important than the function. The most important development that perhaps still needs to occur is for the developers and architects to accept that an 'iconic' building that has 100 per cent vision glazing in this region is a sad waste of energy and our planet's resources, and not to be applauded.

The Way Forward

Efforts are being made in certain areas to respond to the spirit of the changes in legislation and attitude described in this article. Examples such as the Kuwait International Airport designed by Foster + Partners (2011–) reveal aspirations to incorporate sustainable materials and technologies in large-scale building projects. At the urban scale, the Msheireb Properties development in downtown Doha (see pp 92–9 of this issue) is an excellent example of extremely good intentions being translated into effective action.

In the Gulf we have come a very long way in a very short period of time. As a direct result of the speed at which we travelled, we now have a lot to inform us and much that we have learned. We are in a time of consolidation and need to be making sure that the lessons learned are fed back into the process and become part of good practice for designers and contractors. Our focus now needs to be on ensuring the operation of the buildings links fully into the design and construction. And we need to focus on improving our older buildings, because we now have the understanding and capability to take this on. ∆

Gerber Architekten

King Fahad National
Library refurbishment
and extension

Riyadh

Saudi Arabia

2013

right: Gerber Arkitekten won the
competition for the refurbishment
and extension of the King Fahad
National Library in 2003. As
shown in the diagram, the original
library building serves as a central
core and is enclosed by a light
structure that incorporates a three-
dimensional, tensile-stressed steel
cable system to refract light and
provide shading.

opposite top: Interior view of
the King Fahad National Library
showing the space created
between the existing building
and the outer glazed facade
demarcating the addition.
Daylight is distributed throughout
the space by skylights covered by
white membranes.

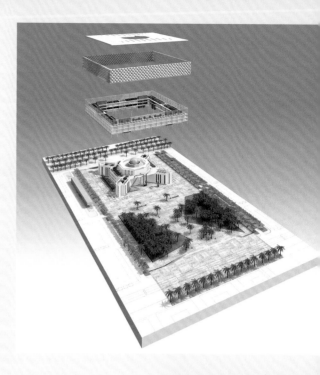

View of the facade of the King Fahad National Library showing the relationship between the tensile shading
system and the glazed curtain wall surrounding the existing building. The facade was combined with a ventilation
and cooling system consisting of layered ventilation and floor cooling to enhance thermal comfort and reduce
energy consumption.

Sheppard Robson

Siemens Middle East
headquarters

Masdar City

Abu Dhabi

UAE

2013

119

below: Parametric analysis informed the design of a lightweight aluminium shading system intended to maximise daylight and views while minimising the amount solar radiation. The project achieved LEED Platinum status and was recognised with a number of awards, including a German Design Council Iconic Award for Corporate Architecture.

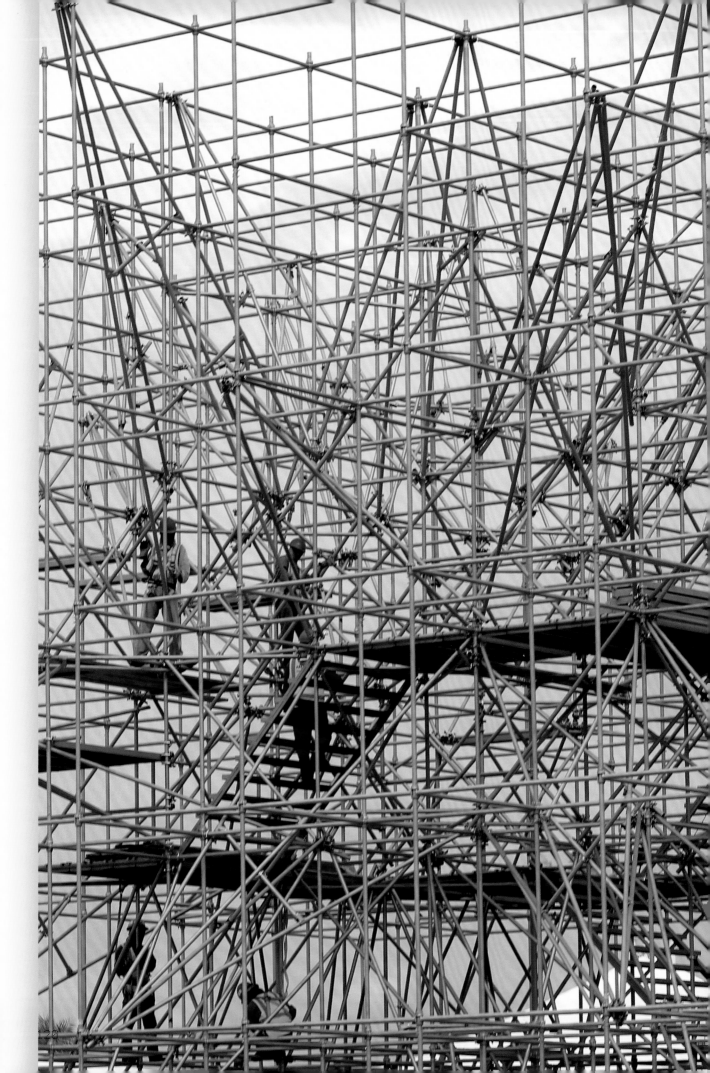

George Katodrytis

Performative Urbanism

An Emerging Model of the Gulf

With the largest stretch of desert sand in the world, the UAE has an extreme climate and arid ecology. Previous to the postwar discovery of oil in the region, the built environment developed with low or no energy to be responsive to extreme climatic changes. Guest-Editor **George Katodrytis** looks at the ways that a more performative approach might be employed in contemporary architecture to make it more culturally and climatically relevant.

Construction workers,
Abu Dhabi,
UAE

From the desert to the making of the new Gulf city – construction workers on scaffolding fabricate a new geometry and facade.

Any discussion about architecture and urbanism in the Gulf is not complete without reference to the region's extreme climate and arid ecology. Paradoxically, prior to the discovery of oil, this harsh but inspiring environment was the setting for small settlements and trading hubs that had survived and flourished since the 19th century surrounded by vast areas of desert. At 84,000 square kilometres (32,450 square miles), the UAE, for example, is one of the world's largest sand deserts stretching from the Gulf coast to the Empty Quarter and east to the Hajar Mountains. Within such territories, Bedouins inherited an ability to endure high temperatures with limited food and water and basic shelter, something unimaginable to the West. They developed the skill and intelligence to navigate, colonise and adapt.[1]

Small coastal settlements were initially formed that were temporary and seasonal, and therefore culture was transient. Yet these early urban patterns developed typologies and materialities that were responsive to climatic changes. This type of urbanism contributed to the shaping of the early traditional Gulf towns made up of *sikkas* (narrow alleyways), high walls, perforated screens, inward-looking houses, inhabited rooftops and abstracted street patterns. Masonry fortress-like buildings with thick walls and generous courtyards utilised wind flow to cool and retain this condition for prolonged periods. Even though this approach has not been adopted in the making of the contemporary Gulf city in recent years, we have witnessed signs of contemporary architecture here embracing new technologies and geometries in order to create buildings that are environmentally responsive.

The early and traditional typology of settlements was consistent across all Gulf towns and remained unchanged until the discovery of oil and the emergence of modernity from the 1950s to the 1970s. This transformation in making the region contemporary was carried out by mainly Western architects who were invited by the various regional rulers to draw plans of their visions. Even though this early modernity was not as pure as its European counterpart, it brought something new: the fusion of a Western modernity of clarity and transparency with local and oriental mystique and intensity of light – a trend that continues today. It is no coincidence that only foreign architects have designed the selected buildings referenced in this article – a hybrid tendency that can be unique in bringing the best of both worlds in terms of global technology and local climate.

John R Harris and Partners,
Sheikh Rashid Tower,
World Trade Centre,
Dubai, UAE,
1979

In 1974, Sheikh Rashid, the ruler of Dubai, commissioned British architect John R Harris to design the 39-storey first modernist tower of Dubai and the tallest building in the Gulf. The elegant facade is made of precast concrete panels.

opposite: His Highness Sheikh Rashid and Her Majesty Queen Elizabeth II accompanied by World Trade Centre architect John R Harris at the building inauguration. This high-profile event demonstrated the symbolic value of Dubai's first tower.

From the 1980s, exposed glass curtain walls were used extensively in the design of almost every commercial and high-rise building facade in the Gulf. This was inevitable given the high land value and rapid influx of investment that created a rush to build projects in a short time. It became the established method of construction, similar to the global real-estate model. Almost any building shape became an airtight glass envelope. At the same time, reclaiming large and arid areas of desert and turning them into livable neighbourhoods is an expensive enterprise both in terms of infrastructure and physical transformation. The combination of fast cities on limited land thus produced a Manhattan-like effect at the end of the 20th century: land division, high-rise building planning and curtain walls.

As this rush to build reached its peak, the building technology of the glass facade in the region remained unchanged. Buildings looked identical. Any discourse on environmental performance and innovation did not exist. The midday heat during summer in the Gulf is quite extreme with temperatures up to 45°C (113°F) and 80 per cent humidity, which is in complete contrast with the desired comfort zone of cool, well-serviced and dust-free interiors. This extreme threshold is perhaps the single most challenging dilemma for the architecture of the region. Such an environment tests all research and application of energy, performative design and technology. The thermal response of any building envelope and geometry in the Gulf can almost alone determine the type of architecture in the region.

On the other hand, at the local and historical context, even after modern urban planning and despite the subsequent introduction of iconic architecture such as the Burj Al Arab and Emirates Towers in the 1990s, the mental map of the Gulf city is still rooted in its Islamic imagery. Among other forms of expression, the city manifests itself as the contemporary interpretation of Orientalism. Urbanism in the Arab world has a remarkable precedent. This is also reflected in the Gulf, such as in the old town centres of Doha, Manama and Dubai. Historically, urbanising large areas and introducing a new aesthetic was very much inherent in the creation of the contemporary Arab city, achieved by connecting small city parts to a larger urban district The absence of any figurative representation in the expression of Islam has generated a unique art form with repetitive patterns of geometric motif. This abstract geometry has many implications, especially in facade treatment, or *mashrabiya*, the screens that once masked the exteriors of buildings.

The work of John R Harris, the architect of the 1979 Sheikh Rashid Tower and World Trade Centre in Dubai, employed this technique through the use of large and repetitive precast concrete panels to wrap the building and protect its interiors from direct sun and heat. This 39-storey building was Dubai's first tower and became the tallest building in the Gulf. It marked the beginning of Sheikh Zayed Road, and a new city had finally been born. Some 30 years later, in 2011 Reiser + Umemoto completed the O-14 Tower in Dubai's Business Bay. In a similar way, the external solid concrete wrapping of this building is both a structure and an environmentally responsive membrane. The white painted exoskeleton stands a metre away from an inner glass-walled enclosure that follows its surface contours. Unlike the dominant curtain-wall facades of the city, O-14 stands out as an alternative modern expression of office design in the Gulf. Its envelope is unmistakably abstract, repetitive, environmental and performative.

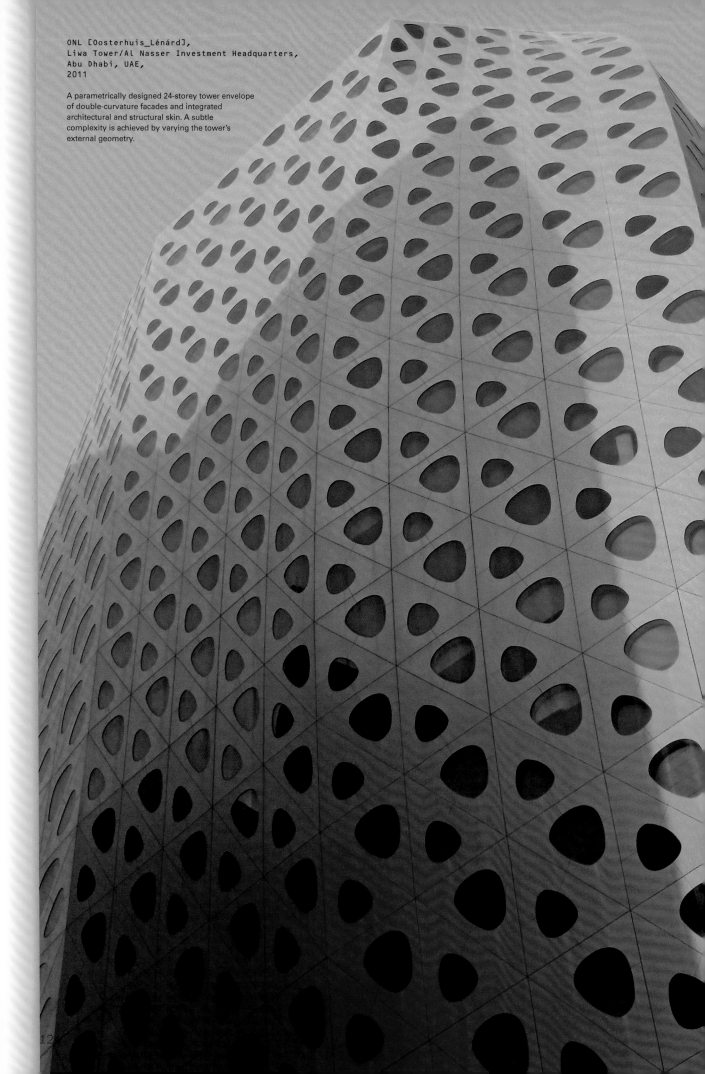

ONL [Oosterhuis_Lénárd],
Liwa Tower/Al Nasser Investment Headquarters,
Abu Dhabi, UAE,
2011

A parametrically designed 24-storey tower envelope
of double-curvature facades and integrated
architectural and structural skin. A subtle
complexity is achieved by varying the tower's
external geometry.

Despite attempts to import Western iconic architectural emblems and figurations, the Islamic city still retains its early abstract character. The lack of figuration in Islam can easily be seen in the urban patterns of the traditional city, interiors of mosques and Arabic calligraphy. The mirage and haziness of the desert point to a system of layers, repetitions and optical illusions. It is therefore possible, using iterations, to generate geometric patterns through new digital tools and scripting iterations. Repetition and differentiation in the contemporary discourse of architecture and its relation to digital replication (repeated modules and panelling) in the Gulf has found a new home. The contemporary city may now, without thematically imitating the past, re-enact tradition and introduce new urban and complex dynamics. Can such interpretation of Orientalism and addressing the abstract rather than the thematic create a shift in direction among international architects, in terms of honing their work to be more culturally relevant in the Gulf?

Reiser + Umemoto,
RUR Architecture,
O-14 Tower,
Dubai, UAE,
2011

The slim structure's dominant feature is an in-situ concrete exoskeleton with 1,326 holes in various sizes. The white painted exoskeleton stands a metre away from an inner glass-walled enclosure that follows its surface contours.

Al Bahr Towers in Abu Dhabi, by Aedas and Arup for the Abu Dhabi Investment Council Headquarters (2012), has pushed envelope adaptability to a new technical efficiency. A dynamic external shading screen has been introduced that reduces solar gain and acts as a moving *mashrabiya*. This external skin comprises umbrella-like units that open and close throughout the day in response to the sun's movements. It has been estimated that this will achieve a 50 per cent reduction in solar gain.

Until recently, westernisation was interpreted as the only form of modernisation in the Gulf. However, contemporary practices and technology can now reinterpret the potential and characteristics of the traditional Arab city without imitating it. Emergent practices of digital and dynamic processes in modelling are capable of incorporating a new language in architecture that can reconnect urbanism to modern life, utilising both environment and culture. Such simulation can address the context and idiosyncrasies found in a locality and make them relevant. This is a new form of modernisation for the region. Instead of celebrating the uniqueness and at times the nostalgic architectural object, this urbanism is based on performance and focuses on how the object (material tectonics), process of production (programmatic iterations) and local behaviour (contextual anomalies) can become culturally significant. The generation of form can now relate to environment and materiality and become indigenous and responsive to fields of influence such as physical forces and environmental dynamics. The Dutch firm ONL [Oosterhuis_Lénárd] designed the Liwa Tower for Al Nasser Investment LLC in Abu Dhabi in 2011. This new headquarters, with its double-curvature facade, integrates architectural geometry with a structural skin and a repetitive pattern of openings in a novel approach to the design of an office building envelope.

Gerber Architekten,
King Fahad National Library
refurbishment and extension,
Riyadh, Saudi Arabia,
2013

below: The facade's white membranes, supported by a tensile-stressed steel cable structure, serve as sunshades and reinterpret traditional patterns with more technologically advanced solutions. The envelope's orientation and design responds directly to the local sun path, combining the required protection from the hot sun with maximum light penetration and transparency.

bottom: Construction details of the metallic skeletal structure facade. The joint and steel-cable component is designed to adjust to various geometries and allow subtle external configurations of the membrane.

Asymptote Architecture,
Yas Viceroy Abu Dhabi Hotel,
Abu Dhabi, UAE,
2009

opposite: The building as a whole performs as an environmentally responsive solution as well as an architecture of spectacle. While the grid shell structure defines the volume, it also serves an environmental purpose by assisting in the stack effect of exiting heated air up and over the facades.

The adoption of abstracted geometry can also address the challenges posed by contemporary representation of Islamic architecture. Rather than using literal Orientalist imagery that tourists expect to find in the Gulf, architecture and interiors can be represented by aura, atmosphere and light, elements that define the oriental in its genuine manifestation. This can be achieved by integrating parametric modelling within the design process. The capacity to design small repeatable components and apply them to a larger governing surface geometry has unlimited potential for environmental and sustainable building, and allows exploration of new types of form. Designing facade systems using adaptability, iterations and geometric configurations allows modelling to control climatic resistance, but also brings a desirable flexibility. Facade layering is a method used in a number of contemporary glass buildings. Similar to the double-facade buildings approach,[2] but with the exterior layer acting as a solar barrier, the skin is made of panellised and shading components to protect against exterior solar gain, but also to reduce interior glare.

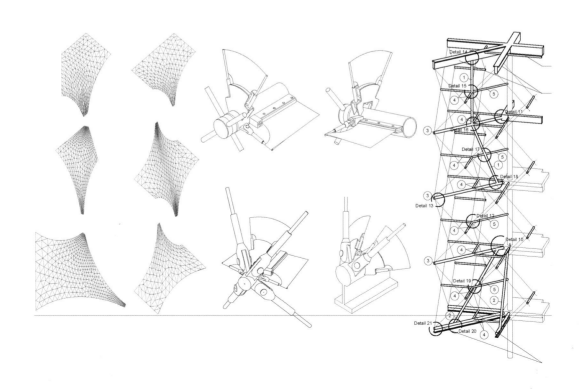

Coating facades with material layers could also provide the possibility of using the resulting cavity areas as buffer zones and as external space. Exterior parametric skin acts as a solar diffusion – like a *mashrabiya* – which can also be layered to create a three-dimensional space of differentiated panels that respond to sun path and wind direction. This layer ultimately refines the profile of the building. It can also be animated, adaptive and interactive to protect further against the intensity of solar impact as well as to adjust the daylighting of the interior. Gerber Architekten's King Fahad National Library refurbishment and extension in Riyadh, Saudi Arabia (2013) and Sheppard Robson's regional headquarters for Siemens (2013) at Foster + Partners' Masdar City in Abu Dhabi employ external building facade white membranes supported by tensile-stressed steel cable structures. Such envelope wrappings introduce new material tectonics and contextualise the buildings environmentally within territories of little or no physical context. Extending this approach further, the Yas Viceroy Abu Dhabi Hotel (2009) by Asymptote Architecture has introduced an architecture that as a whole is both performative, and performs, located within the spectacular setting of the city's Formula 1 racetrack.

Exuberant projects will probably continue to exist in the Gulf, which has become home to some of the world's most controversial settlements – a canvas for global and nomadic crossroads that bisect empty lands of extreme climates and topographies. Within this vast landscape, the city will still strive to redefine itself. Environmental considerations can now, for the first time, challenge the mere iconic and address a new performative and material approach, new abstraction and a new hybrid condition. The emphasis of such exploration is on retaining the city's layering and traditional complexity in an efficient and sustainable manner so that the architecture of the Gulf city may become innovative yet still uncanny and enigmatic. ᴅ

Notes
1. Caline Malek, 'Desert Survival: Secrets of Ancient Bedouin Navigation', *The National*, 26 July 2011: www.thenational.ae/news/uae-news/desert-survival-secrets-of-ancient-bedouin-navigation.
2. Eberhard Oesterle, Rolf-Dieter Lieb, Martin Lutz and Winfried Heusler, *Double-Skin Facades: Integrated Planning*, Prestel (Munich), 2001.

The Struggle for Integrity

Emerging Local Practices in the Gulf

George Katodrytis and Kevin Mitchell

dxb.lab

UAE-based dxb.lab was established in 2000 by principal Khalid Al Najjar, who was joined by Shahab Lutfi as chief executive officer in 2005. Al Najjar was educated at the Southern California Institute of Architecture (SCI-Arc) and then returned to Dubai after studying under Jesse Reiser (Reiser + Umemoto, RUR Architecture) at Columbia University. The practice initially focused on residential projects and has expanded to include larger-scale projects including the 14-storey Code Business Tower, Dubai (2010). The work of dxb.lab is characterised by minimal approaches to form and conceptually clear treatments of material relations.

dxb.lab

Staff Housing

Dubai, UAE

2014

View of the open space defined by a corridor and two linear blocks of the Staff Housing project located in an industrial area of Dubai.

dxb.lab

House 010

Dubai, UAE

2009

opposite top: Facade of House 010 showing the floating solid volume containing private spaces.

Overshadowed by the large-scale and often exaggerated architectural expressions produced by architectural firms with a global reach, the work of local practices in the Gulf has not gained widespread recognition for alternative approaches to the context. Here Guest-Editors **George Katodrytis and Kevin Mitchell** profile the work of four emerging studios – dxb.lab, X-Architects and SHAPE Architecture Practice and Research, based in the UAE, and AGi Architects, with offices in Kuwait and Spain – highlighting the challenges that indigenous studios in the region encounter.

far left: The treatment of vertical structure and horizontal floor and ceiling planes in House 010 is characteristic of dxb.lab's minimalist approach to form.

left: View from the first-floor living areas showing the blurred distinction between interior public space and the courtyard.

Maintaining a critically oriented practice in the Gulf is fraught with challenges, from unbuilt competition-winning entries to cash-flow complications. The limited time for design, the speed of project delivery and the sheer scale of projects often favour larger offices or consortia comprising teams of international consultants with the capacity to negotiate complexity. Additionally, architecture has traditionally been the domain of engineers throughout the broader Middle East and North Africa (MENA) region and the Gulf, and many educational institutions continue to define degrees in terms of 'architectural engineering' or place programmes within engineering faculties. It is therefore no surprise that the production of architecture in the region was inevitably shaped by tendencies and practices that reduced buildings to engineering problems to be solved.

The current situation is not new. The initial wave of development in the Gulf, as early as the 1950s in Kuwait, was also not without what Saba George Shiber described as 'anti-architectural deviations':

> Departing thoroughly from the basic determinants of sound architecture as well as the architectural compulsions of the unique conditions of Kuwait, the strange movement which started around 1955 and reached its zenith in 1964, swamped Kuwait with a bizarre, strangely complicated and humpy architecture that is hard to describe in conventional architectural terms. Perhaps 'modern rococo' comes closest to an identification of the type or 'style' of, especially, modern 'villa' architecture that has come to characterize wide areas of Kuwait and to be the example, par excellence, of modern architectural eclecticism here.[1]

Shiber, and other architects active in what is now the Gulf Cooperation Council (GCC) and neighbouring Iraq, such as Rifat Chadirji, Mohamed Makiya, Hisham Munir, Kamal El Kafrawi and Jafar Tukan, resisted the tendencies towards the 'modern rococo' and struggled earnestly to develop formal strategies and aesthetic expressions that responded to climate and context.

X-Architects

Founded by Ahmed Al-Ali and Farid Esmaeil in 2003 after completing studies the American University of Sharjah (AUS in the UAE, X-Architects initially complet a series of residential and small-scale commercial projects in Dubai.
The practice then expanded into large-scale masterplans that included proposal for sustainable cities (in collaboration wit German-based SMAQ) and schemes for developing housing for UAE nationals. In 2013, X-Architects won a major competiti for the Darb Al Mashaer Masterplan in th centre of Makkah, Saudi Arabia.

X-Architects with BuroHappold

Darb Al Mashaer Masterplan

Makkah, Saudi Arabia

2013

below: Located along a major pilgrimage route, Darb Al Mashaer is a large-scale high-density development that includes hotels, residential units, commercial space and municipal services.

bottom: Darb Al M will provide over 8 square metres (8.6 million square feet of space in a series towers rising from horizontal podium project incorporate a complex network of pedestrian route to accommodate th movement of large numbers of pilgrim

X-Architects with SMAQ,
Johannes Grothaus,
Reflexion and BuroHappold

Xeritown

Dubai, UAE

2007

left: Aerial view of Xeritown, a mixed-use urban development intended to respond to the desert context at architectural and urban scales.

below: Xeritown employs passive strategies at the urban and building scales to mediate the climate, as illustrated in the shading system covering the exterior shopping streets.

Despite the potential difficulties and the challenges that still persist, a number of smaller emerging offices are currently producing work of depth and quality. This article focuses on four practices that can be described as 'indigenous' as the principals are citizens of the countries they are based in or have been resident for an extended period. dxb.lab, X-Architects and SHAPE Architecture Practice and Research, based in the UAE, and AGi Architects, with offices in Kuwait and Spain, have produced projects that represent ways forward in terms of the debate over 'identity' that is often hindered by an emphasis on surface decoration. The practices presented here seem to be less fixated on what buildings may mean, and are more concerned with fundamentally questioning how built form can respond to climate or context-specific socio-cultural norms. Rather than rely on metaphors, emblems or symbols, the practices demonstrate the capacity to question, to abstract and to translate, perhaps because they are more critically aware of what Shiber characterised as 'the basic determinants of sound architecture'. It is also worth noting that those who formed the practices were educated within systems that were more firmly rooted in the discipline of architecture, and some were educated in local educational institutions that have contributed to the development of a distinct architectural culture in the region.

SHAPE

SHAPE Architecture Practice and Resear was established in 2006 by Abdulla Al-Shamsi after completing undergraduate studies at AUS and a graduate degree a Columbia University. Projects have rang from residential buildings to urban desi and infrastructure. As indicated in the Sharjah Housing Master Plan, the firm has focused on developing architectura responses to the particular climate and context of the UAE.

SHAPE Architecture
Practice and Research

Al Sowwah Island Bridge

Abu Dhabi, UAE

2013

Conceived as a linear park containing retail zones and cafes, the proposal for this pedestrian and vehicular bridge provides access to Al Sowwah Island (currently known as Al Maryah Island). The island is intended to be a 114-hectare (281-acre) mixed-use development that will serve as the central business district for Abu Dhabi.

Sharjah Housing
Master Plan

Sharjah, UAE

2013

top: The Sharjah Housing Master
Plan is a proposal for a low-
rise mixed-use neighbourhood
development. Each neighbourhood
cluster contains 200 dwelling
units, a mosque, a community
centre and other amenities.

centre: View of the shaded
pedestrian plaza that serves as
the centre of each neighbourhood
cluster.

Casa V

Sharjah, UAE

2012

Casa V relies on the manipulation
of mass to ensure privacy. Light
and views are controlled through
small punched openings.

These practices have contributed to defining the future of architecture in their home countries. The confident and uncompromising approaches to exemplary projects in Gulf cities in the 1960s and 1970s are once again evident in the work of these young emerging practitioners. In some senses, the same rupture that occurred by devaluing the past and ignoring the value of the local until very recently is also evident when one examines the genealogy of practice in the Gulf. During the late 1990s, the lessons that could have been learned from the deliberate attempts to reconcile place-specific forms of expression with new realities following the discovery of oil and natural gas were ignored in favour of generic buildings with applied motifs.

When examining the work of the practices presented here, it seems that strands of thought that were severed at the turn of the 21st century are being reconnected across a period that was characterised by projects that were bigger but not necessarily better. Surveying the architecture in the Gulf in the 1970s and early 1980s, Udo Kultermann concluded: 'The role of architects in this situation is fragile and ambivalent at the least and a struggle for survival and artistic integrity is taking place. Only future development will show how far and how good the achievements of Arab architects in their own countries will be, and how they will compare with the best of international architects.'[2] While the situation of architects intent on establishing strong locally based practices still remains fragile 40 years later, the work of dxb.lab, X-Architects, SHAPE Architecture Practice and Research, AGi Architects and other emerging practices indicates that progress is possible in the struggle for survival and integrity. ⚇

Notes
1. Saba George Shiber, *The Kuwait Urbanization*, Kuwait Government Printing Office (Kuwait), 1964, p 286.

2. Udo Kultermann, 'Contemporary Arab Architecture: The Architects of the Gulf States', in Hasan-Uddin Khan (ed), *Mimar 14: Architecture in Development*, Concept Media Ltd. (Singapore), 1992, p 57.

AGi Architects

Nasser B Abulhasan (Kuwait) and Joaqu[ín] Pérez-Goicoechea (Spain) established AGi Architects in 2006 after earning advanced degrees at Harvard University. The firm maintains offices in Madrid and Kuwait and is engaged in work in Europe and throughout the Gulf. Early projects completed in Kuwait, such as the Ribbon House (2009), Star House (2009), and M[ ] House (2010) exhibit a formal complexity that relies on the manipulation of intern[al] and external voids to control light and maintain privacy. AGi Architects has recently pursued large-scale projects in Kuwait, such as the Ministry of Interior Affairs General Department of Informati[on] Systems (2013) and the Tamdeen Square Residences (2014).

AGi Architects

Wafra Living

Kuwait City, Kuwait

2011–

The Wafra Living complex relies on setbacks, cuts in the form of subtractions from masses, and veil-like screens to maximise privacy for residential units and common exterior spaces, which include a 'High Square' for tenants at 6 metres (20 feet) above ground level.

i Architects and Bonyan Design

wait Ministry of Interior
fairs General Department of
formation Systems

wait City, Kuwait

13

mpetition-winning entry for the Kuwait
nistry of Interior Affairs General Department
Information Systems building. The design
posal is based on three principles:
oresentativeness, security and functionality.
e main entrance is highlighted by an iconic
wing ribbon of stone.

Inspired by the back-and-forth movement of a mop,
the Mop House is organised around a series of
voids that modulate light, maintain privacy from
neighbours and create enclosed exterior space.
The ground-floor living room and dining room are
opened to the exterior garden.

AGi Architects

Mop House

Al Nuzha, Kuwait

2010

AGi Architects

Tamdeen Square Residences

Kuwait City, Kuwait

2014

Street view of the Tamdeen Square Residences,
a residential complex located in an area planned
for urban development in the south of Kuwait
City. AGi Architects' proposal is comprised of six
90-unit towers extending from an elevated plinth
containing parking.

A Field of Possibilities

The Post-Oil Future of Bahrain

NOURA AL SAYEH

Diplomatic area

Manama

Bahrain

2008–

Aerial view of the Diplomatic area and centre of Manama that clearly shows the different layers of urban development of the city, from the dense neighbourhoods of historical Manama, to the government headquarters planned in the 1970s and 1980s, to the more recent developments on reclaimed land along the coast.

COUNTERPOINT
01/2015
No 233
△D

Much of the continuing urban development of the Gulf region rests on the oil economy. What happens, though, when the oil runs out? What is the alternative model? Bahrain is already facing the depletion of the oil that supported its rapid growth. **Noura Al Sayeh**, the Head of Architectural Affairs at the Ministry of Culture of the Kingdom of Bahrain, highlights how architecture might be developed to generate new urban forms that are economically viable and environmentally sustainable.

At first glance, the urban landscape of Bahrain appears similar to most of its Gulf neighbours: a healthy scattering of new high-rises, sail-shaped buildings, malls disguised and replicating city centres, and gated residential compounds, all seemingly randomly arranged along engineered coastlines and connected by an imposing infrastructure of highways, tunnels and bridges weaving through the flat landscape. However, present-day Bahrain faces unique challenges that distinguish it from other countries in the region, such as the depletion of the oil that supported its rapid growth. Whereas the island led the Gulf into the age of oil-based economies prior to the Second World War, it now has the potential to lead it out with the cultivation of the appropriate development policies.

The Past that Made the Present
As cities tend to develop in relation to the industries and economic forces that finance them, the oil industry has produced cities where, more so than in other places, the price of energy has never been factored in as a finite resource. The urban landscape of Bahrain has therefore largely developed under the logic of cheap oil, encouraging the dominance of the car as the preferred mode of transportation and resulting in a heavy infrastructure of roads that dominates the form of the landscape. On the face of it, Bahrain can resemble Doha, Dubai, Kuwait City and also to some extent Houston and Baku.

The initial phases of development following the discovery of oil in 1932, and the subsequent independence of the state of Bahrain in 1973, corresponded to a clear Modernist agenda; on newly reclaimed lands, the tabula rasa context became home to free-standing buildings freed from the ground plane and supported by pilotis. This development represented a strong contrast to Manama's existing dense urban fabric – a maze of courtyard houses connected by a network of small shaded streets. Compactness gave way to singular buildings of a much larger scale from the mid-1970s, reflecting a bold confidence inspired by the oil economy. These buildings, mostly government headquarters

OFFICE Kersten Geers David Van Severen	Amwaj Islands
Dar Jinaa	Muharraq
Muharraq	Bahrain
Bahrain	2002–
2014	

top: Located in the dense historic neighbourhood of Muharraq, Dar Jinaa is a small music house that negotiates the thresholds of privacy and public space through a wire-mesh facade that can be lifted up for special occasions, opening the ground floor of the building to the public.

bottom: Aerial view of the land reclamation for the Amwaj Islands off the coast of Muharraq. The man-made islands were the first planned residential community that offered freehold landownership for expatriates, and were completely disconnected from the existing urban fabric.

ministries, were not only large, but were separated by
...nses of space that resulted in much lower densities than
... of the inner city.
...he legacy of the oil-based economy led to the erasure
... specificities of local, natural environment and cultural
...ing traditions. The matrix of skyscrapers, controlled
...ior environments, extensive highways and gated
...munities, common to all Gulf cities at the beginning
... 21st century, was superimposed upon existing
...itions. Though some traces of the past remained, the
...ent took precedence. Even the famed sweet water
...gs were gradually lost to rapid urban development and
...ging that began soon after the discovery of oil.

...arios for a Future Without Oil

...e Bahrain shares many similarities with the other
...states, it is also facing some very specific challenges.
...gh it may have been the first in the region to have
...overed oil, Bahrain now has the lowest reserves of all
...Cooperation Council (GCC) countries: it has 125 million
...els of proven crude oil reserves (0.03 per cent of the GCC
...rves, and 0.01 per cent of world crude oil reserves), and
...oducing only 49,000 barrels a day.[1] This situation gives
...o questions about the future. For example, how will
...ain continue to develop and sustain itself financially
...out petroleum supplies? Certainly the government
...aking great strides in pursuing a policy of economic
...rsification. For example, Bahrain was the first Gulf state
...plement a Free Trade Agreement (FTA) with the US in
...ust 2006. Its second export after oil is aluminium, and it
...petes with Malaysia as a worldwide centre for Islamic
...king. At present, though, Bahrain's economy continues
... heavily dependent on oil: petroleum production and
...ing account for more than 60 per cent of its export
...ipts, 70 per cent of government revenues, and 11
...cent of GDP.[2] How might long-term economic shifts,
...ever, play out in the built environment? Might a future
...out petroleum also mean a move away from the logic
... Oil City, and responding instead to the new reality of
...easing scarcity of resources, both oil and water? Could
...also dictate new urban forms that are economically and
...ronmentally sustainable?
...t is not only depleting natural resources and the
...nomy's dependence on them that present a challenge
...Bahrain. It is a small country with a finite amount of
...l – 717 square kilometres (277 square miles) spread over
...ain of 30 islands[3] – and with a fast-growing population.
...ording to the Central Informatics Organisation (CIO) 2010
...sus, its population nearly doubled between 2001 and
..., from 0.66 million to 1.22 million, an annual average
...vth rate of 7.4 per cent.[4] This makes Bahrain one of the
...st densely inhabited countries in the world. With a limited
...unt of available space and the problems associated with
...tinuing to reclaim land from the sea, growth must occur
...in existing urbanised areas.

While this type of infill development, mostly
concentrated around the urban centres of Manama and
Muharraq, cannot accommodate large-scale real-estate
projects – a key component of the post-oil economy
diversification initiatives – it would encourage more efficient
use of the country's scarce land resources and elevate the
general quality of the urban fabric. This would result in
better integration and act as a catalyst for the improvement
of the public realm. New developments of larger size
would continue to develop on the large stocks of available
reclaimed lands and pockets of barren land left on the
outskirts of and between the dense urban matrix, continuing
to exist as another juxtaposed urban form.

Beyond the dichotomy of old and new, where
architecture oscillates between nostalgic depictions of an
idealised past and a bold bet on an over-optimised future,
projects within an existing urban context are obliged to
consider the contemporary urban matrix, and building within
these constraints brings the question of local identity to the
fore. In an increasingly intertwined world, with industrialised
production methods and imported materials, what does it
mean to be local, and how can a specific architecture be
created? Does it make sense to resort to foreign architects
while seeking to be local? Amidst a region with a growing
identity crisis, what should be the characteristics of a
contemporary and site-specific architecture? Projects
commissioned by the Ministry of Culture have attempted to
tackle these questions though initiatives aimed at rehabilitating
the historic neighbourhoods of Manama and Muharraq.

The Khalefeyah Library (2014), by SeARCH Architects, for
example, is a small three-storey community library located
in Muharraq. Situated on a very small plot within this dense
neighbourhood, the project employs a series of cantilevered
volumes that reference the footprints of buildings that were
located on this very plot at different periods. It makes the
past visible by exposing urban layers that had been traced,
erased and re-traced over time.

Dar Al Riffa Al Odah and Dar Jinaa (2014), two music
houses by OFFICE Kersten Geers David Van Severen, are
located in East Riffa and Muharraq respectively. Similar in
form, instead of sharing a courtyard both are conceived as
a stacking of three identical floor plates, and therefore still
relate to the repetitive rooms of traditional Bahraini homes.
The outer facades consist of a wire mesh over glazing. The
mesh layer functions as a shading device for the outdoor
circulation space created between the wire frame and the
glass enclosure.

The Pearling, Testimony of an Island Economy urban
project, Bahrain's second inscription to the UNESCO World
Heritage List, comprises a series of 16 monuments to the
pearling industry, connected within the old neighbourhoods
of Muharraq by an urban pathway. Also designed by OFFICE
Kersten Geers David Van Severen, in collaboration with
Bureau Bas Smets, Pearl Squares (2013) is envisaged as a
linear route that links 19 small public places constructed
on empty plots of land where buildings were recently

SeARCH

Al Khalefeyah Library

Muharraq

Bahrain

2014

The three cantilevering floors of the library refer to the footprint of previous buildings, revealing the urban layers of this historical neighbourhood.

OFFICE Kersten Geers David Van Severen

Dar Al Riffa Al Odah

East Riffa

Bahrain

2014

Conceived as a smaller 'brother' to the Dar Jinaa, the Dar Al Riffa is conceived as an annexe to the existing coral-stone historical Dar of Riffa. Its position towards the Dar creates a courtyard between the two buildings that can be used for outdoor musical performances.

ICE Kersten Geers David Van Severen
  Bureau Bas Smets

rl Squares

arraq

rain

3

ries of small public spaces within the dense
hbourhoods of Muharraq, the squares are located on
s where buildings were recently destroyed to make way
igher buildings. The street lights and trees are placed on
d, re-creating the built mass of the previous building.

ries of climatic devices such as underfloor cooling
ems, humidity walls and water fountains are included
ie squares to create microclimates that make the spaces
fortable in the warmer and humid summer months.

demolished. Here, instead of infilling the vacant land with buildings, the architects proposed green public spaces that rely on a series of climatic devices (underfloor cooling, public fountains and water walls) to create microclimates that encourage their use even during the hot summer months. The project compensates for the lack of open areas within the dense neighbourhoods of Muharraq and creates genuine urban public spaces and passages within the context of the Gulf city.

Although these projects are small in size and minimal in their impact on the urban fabric, it is hoped that they will set an example for contextual architecture that makes the most of the existing urban situation, and introduces design principles that take into consideration social, cultural and climatic factors without resorting to a pastiche of the past or a utopian projection of the future. In doing so, they contribute to defining and articulating a contemporary local architectural identity that addresses the specifics of place.

In Between the Possible and the Plausible

One could optimistically view the urban landscape of Bahrain as a continuous field of urban figures connected by an efficient infrastructure that indiscriminately encompasses the good, the bad and the ugly as well as the old, the preserved and the new. Rather than looking towards Dubai as the model for urbanism in the Gulf, cities could seek to emulate Tokyo, where the strength of the urban form is not derived from individual buildings, but from the quality of the public spaces and the streets that connect them. The challenge will be to improve the quality of the interstitial spaces that accommodate life in the city, and it will be up to the public sector to invest the appropriate resources to achieve this. Hopefully, promoting smaller-scale contextual and sustainable infills within this matrix will in time raise the quality of the urban fabric on the whole.

At the other end of the spectrum, in a slightly more apocalyptic yet relatively plausible scenario, Bahrain could risk sharing the fate of Nauru, the first country to have been annihilated by capitalist forces. Having discovered phosphate in the early 1900s, this South Pacific island had the highest GDP per capita income from the 1960s to the early 1970s. After reserves were depleted, the country's wealth disappeared and its environment and economy were destroyed.

The threat of depletion of resources such as oil, water and land in Bahrain calls for innovation, reinvention, and a reconsideration of its specific social and cultural context. Through small and innovative urban interventions, Bahrain has the potential to demonstrate how architecture and urbanism can respond to post-oil conditions that will ultimately affect the Gulf region as a whole. Between Tokyo and Nauru lies a field of possibilities. ⌂

Notes
1. Figures drawn from Bahrain country profile, Gulf Base, 29 August 2014: www. gulfbase.com/Gcc/Index/4.
2. Bahrain country profile, Forbes, December 2013: www.forbes.com/places/bahrain/.
3. Bahrain country profile, Aljazeera, February 2011: www.aljazeera.com/news/2011/02/2011216721134766490.html
4. *Kingdom of Bahrain Economic Yearbook,* Economic Development Board, 2013, p 13: www.bahrainedb.com/en/EDBDocuments/Bahrain-Economic-Yearbook.pdf.

ARCHITECTURAL DESIGN

UAE AND THE GULF

CONTRIBUTORS

Ameena Ahmadi holds the position of Architecture Manager at the Qatar Foundation where she is involved in managing Education City's masterplan and facilities. Additionally, she has been working with a multidisciplinary team on the Foundation's Karama Initiative, with the goal of positively transforming standards of quality of life for all migrant workers involved in Foundation activities. She is also an active member of the Doha Architecture Forum, an informal association with the aim of sharing knowledge and establishing a critical discourse on architecture and the built environment in Doha via talks and discussions. She has a Bachelor of Architecture degree from the American University of Sharjah, UAE, and a Master's of Science in Advanced Architectural Studies from University College London (UCL).

Terri Meyer Boake is a professor in the School of Architecture at the University of Waterloo in Ontario. She is a researcher for the Canadian Institute of Steel Construction. Publications include: *Understanding Steel Design: An Architectural Design Manual* (Birkhäuser, 2012), *Diagrid Structures: Systems, Connections, Details* (Birkhäuser, 2014) and *Architecturally Exposed Structural Steel* (Birkhäuser, 2015). She has lectured worldwide on applications in architecturally exposed structural steel. She is a member of the Skyscraper Center Editorial Board for the Council on Tall Buildings and Urban Habitat (CTBUH).

Robert Cooke is a doctor of engineering and a chartered energy engineer. He is a board member of the Emirates Green Building Council through which he is helping to build links with academia and promote knowledge sharing and awareness across the industry. At Buro Happold he has worked on projects across the globe and led a range of new initiatives from cutting-edge research to the development of new tools for improving sustainability. He was awarded Middle East Engineer of the Year for 2013 at the Middle East Architect Awards, and MEP Engineer of the Year for 2012 at the Middle East MEP Awards.

Adam Himes is an architect and researcher based in Istanbul. He has been published in *CLOG* and has participated in research projects in Doha, Pittsburgh and Boston. As a research associate at Carnegie Mellon University, he led the research and content development of the 4dDoha:Buildings and Pittsburgh Projects apps. His research examining the future of cities formed the basis of *Projections* an installation exhibited in Boston and Los Angeles.

Kelly Hutzell is an educator and a registered architect with a focus on urban design. She is an Associate Teaching Professor at Carnegie Mellon University, with appointments on the Pittsburgh and Doha campuses. She is co-principal investigator of 4dDoha, an ongoing research project examining Doha's architectural and urban growth. Her research interests include sustainable urbanism, rapidly developing cities, and the intersection of urban design, information design and interactive design.

Mona El Mousfy has held a full-time position at the College of Architecture, Art and Design, American University of Sharjah, since 2002. She is the senior architect for the Sharjah Art Foundation Art Spaces and the last five editions of the Sharjah Biennial. Her design studio, space_continuum, focuses on 20th-century cultural spaces and their relation across scale and programme.

Todd Reisz is an architect and writer currently focusing on the cities of the Gulf region, from both historical and contemporary perspectives. He was editor of *Al Manakh 2: Gulf Continued* (April 2010) which analyses the recent developments of cities in Saudi Arabia, Kuwait, Qatar, Bahrain and the UAE. He is currently appointed the Daniel Rose Visiting Assistant Professor in Urbanism at Yale University School of Architecture.

Varkki Pallathucheril is a professor and interim dean in the College of Architecture, Art and Design at the American University of Sharjah where he teaches in the Master of Urban Planning Program. His scholarly interests include computer applications in urban planning and design, as well as urban planning, urban design and urban form in the UAE.

Rami el Samahy is an educator and practitioner of architecture and urban design. An Associate Teaching Professor at Carnegie Mellon University, he holds joint appointments between the campuses in Pittsburgh, Pennsylvania and Doha, Qatar. He is also a founding partner of over,under, an award-winning multidisciplinary studio with projects in the Middle East, Central America and the US.

Noura Al Sayeh is an architect who graduated from the École Polytechnique Fédérale de Lausanne. She has worked in Jerusalem, New York and Amsterdam, and has been the Head of Architectural Affairs at the Ministry of Culture of the Kingdom of Bahrain since 2009. She has also curated several exhibitions of Bahrain's National Participations at the 2010 and 2012 Venice Biennale.

Sharmeen Syed is an architect and researcher. She has been design architect for the Sharjah Art Foundation's Art Spaces project, and was a production architect for the Sharjah Biennials 10 and 11. Her studio, logue: praxis/broadcast, is engaged in trans-disciplinary projects and extended realms of design.

Steven Velegrinis is the Director of Urban Design for Perkins+Will in Dubai. He is an urban planner and landscape architect with almost 20 years' experience in Australia, Asia and the Middle East. He is also an Adjunct Professor of Urban Design at the American University of Sharjah. He grew up in Australia and pursued a career in urban planning and heritage conservation before embarking on a career in landscape architecture. Influenced by his multi-disciplinary background, his work has attempted to promote a more instrumental role for the landscape as an organising medium in urban planning. His recent work and research seek to promote the idea of landscape urbanism as the future for sustainable urban development in the Middle East and Asia.

Sarina Wakefield originally studied archaeology at the University of Leicester, gaining a BSc in 2001. She then went on to gain an MA in Museum Studies in 2004, also from the University of Leicester. She has since worked on museum and heritage projects in the UK and the Kingdom of Bahrain. She has published journal and book articles relating to museum development and falconry in the UAE. She is currently pursuing a PhD, full time, entitled 'Franchising Heritage: The Creation of a Transnational Heritage Industry in the Emirate of Abu Dhabi'. She is also responsible for organising the 'Museums in Arabia' Conference.

Jeffrey Willis is a mechanical engineer with more than 40 years' experience in the construction industry. He has been working for Arup for 35 years, being located at various times in offices in Europe, the Middle East and the Far East, involved in a variety of projects from individual building design to masterplanning, and in commercial, industrial, and transportation and infrastructure design. He is currently based in Dubai, as Sustainability Leader for Arup in the Gulf. He is the Arup representative as a Founder Member of the Emirates Green Building Council, and holds the position of the Emirates GBC's Vice-Chairman of the Emirates Green Building Council. He has represented both Arup and the Emirates GBC at international conferences on sustainable building design, and has lectured at universities in Singapore and the UAE.

What is Architectural Design?

Founded in 1930, *Architectural Design* (Δ) is an influential and prestigious publication. It combines the currency and topicality of a newsstand journal with the rigour and production qualities of a book. With an almost unrivalled reputation worldwide, it is consistently at the forefront of cultural thought and design.

Each title of Δ is edited by an invited guest-editor, who is an international expert in the field. Renowned for being at the leading edge of design and new technologies, Δ also covers themes as diverse as architectural history, the environment, interior design, landscape architecture and urban design.

Provocative and inspirational, Δ inspires theoretical, creative and technological advances. It questions the outcome of technical innovations as well as the far-reaching social, cultural and environmental challenges that present themselves today.

For further information on Δ, subscriptions and purchasing single issues see:

www.architectural-design-magazine.com

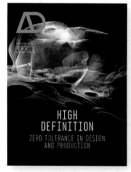

Volume 84 No 1
ISBN 978 1118 451854

Volume 84 No 2
ISBN 978 1118 452721

Volume 84 No 3
ISBN 978 1118 535486

Volume 84 No 4
ISBN 978 1118 522530

Volume 84 No 5
ISBN 978 1118 613481

Volume 84 No 6
ISBN 978 1118 663301